CHICAGO
CALAMITIES

CHICAGO CALAMITIES

DISASTER IN THE WINDY CITY

GAYLE SOUCEK
ILLUSTRATIONS BY BRIAN DISKIN

THE
History
PRESS

All images courtesy of the author's collection unless otherwise specified.

First published 2010

ISBN 978-1-5402-2098-1

Soucek, Gayle.
Chicago calamities : disaster in the Windy City / Gayle Soucek ; with illustrations by Brian Diskin.
p. cm.
ISBN 978-1-5402-2098-1
1. Disasters--Illinois--Chicago--History. 2. Chicago (Ill.)--History. I. Title.
F548.3.S74 2010
977.3'11--dc22
2010040434

Notice: The information in this book is true and complete to the best of our knowledge. It is offered without guarantee on the part of the author or The History Press. The author and The History Press disclaim all liability in connection with the use of this book.

This book is dedicated to all whose lives were snuffed out too soon by an act of God or man.

Requiescat in pace, *Debi, Steve and Roger.*

CONTENTS

CONTENTS

Part V: Riots and Anarchy

INTRODUCTION

If you can't explain it simply, you don't understand it well enough.

—Albert Einstein

Researching history is sort of like putting together a jigsaw puzzle with some missing—and some extra—pieces. Sometimes the image is almost complete, but none of the remaining parts fit neatly into the open spaces. When that happens, the best one can do is draw a logical line to fill in the missing brushstrokes and hope that the final picture accurately represents what was intended.

Take, for example, the sinking of the SS *Eastland*. According to various accounts, the ship was carrying *exactly* 2,573 passengers and crew. Or 2,753. Or perhaps it was 3,200. And although almost all reports agree that precisely 844 souls perished in the tragedy, a respected newspaper of the day quoted an official on the scene who claimed that more than 900 bodies had been recovered and that they hadn't yet breached the hull. Official records from authorities such as the coroner's office can be incomplete or inaccurate, especially for disasters that happened long ago. In some cases, entire families were wiped out; who was left to complain if little Billy or Uncle Joe weren't counted? As Lenin once said, "A lie told often enough becomes the truth."

Eyewitness accounts aren't any more reliable. Many years ago, I had the honor of meeting a survivor from the tragic Our Lady of the Angels fire at a writers' conference. She shared with me a horrifying personal memory of watching a friend burn to death in front of her very eyes. I carried that conversation close to my heart, knowing that if I ever wrote about the tragedy someday that I had been gifted with a tiny shard of the shattered memories of that day. As I wrote this book, I routinely flipped through the impersonal casualty lists from the fire, only to discover that the friend's name was not recorded under the fatalities. Actually, no one with the exact name was listed as even being in that specific classroom.

Was my acquaintance lying? Of course not. Perhaps the child went by a more casual nickname. There was a similar name in a different classroom. Perhaps in the confusion, children from one room somehow made it to another nearby class in an attempt to escape the beastly inferno. Perhaps my colleague, severely burned and near death herself, was confused about whom had met such a tragic fate just seconds before rescue. Most likely, the historical records are in error. I will never know, because the brave woman died of her long-ago injuries shortly after we met.

With this in mind, please forgive any perceived discrepancies between my accounts and others; in all cases, I have struggled to quote the most reliable sources. I hope once you read this book, you will walk away with some empathy for the victims' suffering and a sense of the cultural significance of these disasters. If you do, then I have met my goal.

Part I
FLAMES OF HELL

The Great Chicago Fire

Nobody could see it all—no more than one man could see the whole of the Battle of Gettysburg. It was too vast, too swift, too full of smoke, too full of danger, for anybody to see it all...It was simply indescribable in its terrible grandeur.

—Horace White, editor in chief, Chicago Tribune

The autumn of 1871 had been one of the driest in memory, the tail-end of a vicious drought that had gripped Chicago and the Great Lakes area since midsummer. Between July and October, only a scant 2.5 inches of rain had fallen on the parched city, a mere trifle in comparison with the normal average of about 14.0 inches for the period. Small fires scampered through the dusty streets, taunting the exhausted men of the fire department who chased them with a mixture of determination and despair. There were too many of them—about twenty in the first week of October alone—and too few resources to bring to bear against the incessant flames. Something had to give.

Everything was as dry as a tinderbox. The city itself was, at that time, a city of wood. Hastily erected tenements of board and log crouched along every avenue. Wooden sidewalks helped pedestrians avoid the usually muddy and swampy streets, the byproduct of building a town on top of a marsh. But now, those streets were as dry as a bone. The unseasonably hot autumn

Engraving of the Chamber of Commerce Building before the fire.

winds swirled dry leaves and dirt in miniature cyclones across the rutted wagon trails, and passing carriages left billowing clouds of dust and grit in their wakes. As people ambled along, twigs crackled and snapped underfoot. Many covered their faces with handkerchiefs, their eyes smarting and lungs burning from the perpetual haze of acrid smoke that hung over the city like a blanket.

On the evening of Sunday, October 8, Patrick and Catherine O'Leary and their five children had retired early for the night. Their modest wood-frame home was located at 137 De Koven Street on Chicago's near southwest side, in a working-class neighborhood of mostly poor Irish immigrants. The house actually consisted of two small adjoining cottages, and the O'Learys rented the front two-room cottage to the McLaughlin family. In the rear, bordering a small alley, was a barn in which Catherine O'Leary kept her

People flee over wooden bridges across the Chicago River as the fire approaches. The river did not stop the fire, as expected.

livestock. The six cows, one calf and horse and wagon were her livelihood—and the only appreciable wealth her family owned.

Shortly before 9:00 p.m. that night, a neighbor, Daniel Sullivan, banged on their door to warn them that the barn was on fire. Sullivan had a wooden leg and was known to his neighbors and friends as "Peg Leg." He claimed that he had been sitting against a neighbor's fence on De Koven Street when he spotted the fire in O'Leary's barn. According to his later testimony, he ran to the barn in order to rescue the animals and then rushed to awaken the family. He managed to rescue the calf and released one cow that fled and was never found, but the other animals were trapped.

The O'Learys raced to see if they could save anything, but the barn was completely aflame. Meanwhile, the McLaughlins had a small party going on that evening in front of their cottage, and everyone joined in a quick effort to gather buckets of water. It was too late for the barn, but the bucket brigade kept pouring water on the cottages and managed to keep the fire at bay while someone ran down the street to a nearby pharmacy to pull the fire alarm. The first alarm box did not activate, and the neighbor ran off in search of another.

In the meantime, a fire spotter in the courthouse tower to the north spotted the flames and pulled an alarm. From his perspective, however, he misjudged the location and sent crews in a wild scramble about a mile southwest of the actual fire. By the time the first engines arrived on the

Ruins of the courthouse after the fire. Prisoners in the basement were released to flee for their lives.

scene, the fire was out of control. It spared the O'Learys' humble cottages but sped to the northeast, aiming directly for the heart of the city. At that point, no one knew the monster they were facing.

The previous day, a massive fire at a wood mill and lumberyard on South Canal Street had exhausted and depleted fire department resources. A hook and ladder unit was destroyed in the blaze, along with hoses and other equipment. The seventeen-hour battle pushed men nearly to their breaking points, but their heroic efforts prevailed and the fire was snuffed out. Now, without a decent night's rest, they were facing an even larger conflagration. To make matters worse, the coal needed to stoke the pumping steamers was in short supply. Desperate fireman began to rip up boards from the wooden sidewalks to fuel the pumpers, while others raced on foot the several blocks to the engine house to retrieve a few precious buckets of coal.

The fire, however, would not wait. The brisk twenty-mile-per-hour southwest breeze whipped the flames from building to building, incinerating everything in sight. At first, people believed that the fire would stop when it reached the south branch of the Chicago River, but it hopped across the river with ease, its fierce embers dancing across the wooden ships moored in the water. Next, the inferno raged through Conley's Patch, a shantytown of poor immigrants living in crowded wooden shacks near the river. It was past midnight now, and many of the residents had little if any warning of the fiery death headed for their humble doors.

The insatiable blaze, fueled by kindling, hay and the common wood shavings often used by the poor as an inexpensive alternative to coal, now developed a life of its own. It had grown strong enough to create its own intense updraft, creating a vacuum effect that drew cooler air and fuel into the base of the fire. Known as the convection effect, this phenomenon allowed the fire to advance like a whirlwind without any assistance from the gusty breezes that had earlier aided its movement. After it quickly dispatched the mills and factories in its path, it bore down on the city center of commerce and administration.

As it approached the courthouse, workers scrambled to rescue vital records. There was no time to safely evacuate the one hundred or so prisoners locked up in the basement jail, so deputies tossed open the cells and instructed the inmates to flee. Just five convicted murderers remained in custody, moved by police to a safer location. Only moments later, the massive bell in the courthouse tower came crashing through the ceiling and fell all the way through to the basement

By this time, a stampede of thousands of terrified residents surged toward the perceived safety of the north division. Some were trampled in the crush of bodies, and families and children became separated in the chaos. Merchants, bankers and others who could afford it bartered with wagon drivers to carry precious belongings or inventory out of the fire's path. The honest drivers were heroes; the dishonest ones were pirates who demanded an unreasonable sum of cash upfront, only to dump the cargo in the street as soon as another unfortunate soul sought to engage them.

Some businesses were fortunate enough to have their own stables. Field & Leiter, the predecessor to Chicago's iconic Marshall Field & Company, was able to save millions of dollars in valuable inventory through the heroic efforts of its teams of drivers, who galloped through the smoke and flames to deposit hastily salvaged merchandise at a safe spot along the lakefront. At first, it seemed as though the elegant building at State and Madison might

Residents wandered about in shock, surveying the ash-covered ruins.

be saved as well. Employees and the principals slaved throughout the night wielding pumps and hoses, even as the fire raged around them. At about 1:30 a.m., the gaslights flickered out, but they resolutely continued to work by candlelight and by the orange glow from the omnipresent flames. By about 3:30 a.m., the waterworks to the north of downtown fell to the hungry flames, and soon the city's water mains ran dry. Now there was no means left to fight the fire, which was finishing off the business section and marching on to the north division. Field & Leiter's beautiful marble palace eventually collapsed in flames in the wee hours of the morning, just as the last employees fled from the building with singed hair and soot-smudged faces.

Earlier that morning, the blaze had threatened the South Side Gas Works. A courageous engineer quickly diverted the gas to reservoirs and sewers and shut down the plant. Although it did explode and burn, the employee's

The business and financial district was reduced to rubble.

bravery prevented an explosion of epic proportions. By this time, it has been estimated that as many as nine separate fires were raging in tandem. It was virtually impossible to tell what was happening, as the fire was so vast that no one person could view it as a whole. Instead, historians have attempted to piece together hundreds of eyewitness accounts into a coherent picture. Although enlightening, it does make the sequence of events somewhat muddied in the historical record.

All accounts, however, seem to agree on one point: the terrified crush of humanity that fled ahead of the flames was heart-rending but sometimes dangerous and unstable. The tragedy brought out the best in some, the worst in others. Looters and drunkards joined the crowds, attacking the helpless and pillaging from the businesses. In some reports, there are tales of thieves smashing windows and stealing merchandise, only to throw it in the street or willfully destroy their spoils. The night was a kaleidoscope of courage and cowardice, integrity and dishonesty and selfishness and selflessness.

The fire continued to burn unabated until it finally began to tire late in the day on Monday. It had simply run out of fuel as it burned to the end of the north district and reached the dry sod of the prairie. Shortly after midnight, during the early morning hours of Tuesday, October 10, a belated rainfall fell on the scorched earth and snuffed out the last stragglers of flame.

In its wake, the once proud young city resembled a Martian landscape. About one-third of the city's residents—nearly ninety thousand people—were left homeless. They huddled along the lakefront or in the prairies to the west and north, hungry and thirsty. There was no food and precious little potable water. In most cases, they had lost almost all of their worldly belongings. Even those who had been able to salvage a few items often lost them to thieves or trampling crowds; now all they had were the clothes on their backs. Class and social status no longer mattered. Millionaires wandered in shock along with laborers and immigrants. Most of those whose homes were spared opened their doors to the refugees, sharing whatever they had with friends and strangers alike.

Actually, they were the lucky ones—they had survived. About three hundred people lost their lives in the conflagration, although the exact number has never been determined. In some cases, entire families had been wiped out. With the nearest relatives still in Ireland or Germany or Scandinavia, those poor souls simply disappeared into the flames, leaving family in the mother country to wonder what had become of their kin in America.

The business district was crowded with buildings made of wood and stone.

The financial impact was also devastating. The fire caused about $222 million in property loss, about one-third of the city's total valuation. The swath of destruction spread for four miles, from DeKoven (1100 South) north to Fullerton (2400 North) and west to about Canal (500 West). More than two thousand acres were charred and blackened, with just rubble and debris where a great city had once stood. The only thing the fire did not destroy was Chicago's spirit.

Almost immediately, the rebuilding started. Donations began to pour in from across the country, and workers hammered together temporary dwellings for the homeless. The city, however, would not make the same mistake twice. Business and civic leaders quickly convened with fire safety crusaders and insurance investigators to develop fire and building codes that would make Chicago one of the most fire-safe cities in America. The resulting regulations changed the very face of the business district.

Field & Leiter opened a new store just two weeks later in an old horse barn that it hastily refurbished for the purpose. Shortly thereafter, the company built a sturdy brick warehouse and showroom for its wholesale trade, while its retail division remained in the horse barn until a suitable retail location could be found. Never again would the two divisions be housed together, because insurance companies could not afford the exposure of insuring such an expensive enterprise.

That autumn, a perpetual haze of smoke from many small fires hung in the air.

Hotelier and business leader Potter Palmer had opened a beautiful new hotel, the Palmer House, just thirteen days before the fire. It was (for its brief life) the tallest in the city, towering eight stories above the street. Its interior was decorated with white Italian marble, and French chandeliers cast a warm glow on the hallways and lobby. He had built it as a wedding present in honor of his wife, Bertha, and it promised to be the most elegant lodging the city had to offer. The fire, however, reduced it to rubble. Palmer, undeterred, immediately set to work on an even grander, and this time fireproof, hotel.

Palmer was so certain of his post-fire inn that he dared anyone to prove him wrong. He challenged curiosity seekers or aspiring arsonists to attempt to set the hotel ablaze in an advertisement:

> *If at the expiration of* [one hour], *the fire does not spread beyond the room, the person accepting this invitation is to pay for all damages done and for the use of the room. If the fire does extend beyond the room (I claim it will not), there shall be no charge for the damage done.*

Luckily, no one ever accepted Palmer's challenge, and the Palmer House Hotel (now part of the Hilton chain) remains a landmark to this day. Despite the crippling odds, Chicago itself rose from the ashes like the legendary phoenix. Just twenty-two years later, the city dazzled visitors when it hosted the World's Columbian Exposition, removing any doubt that it was indeed a world-class metropolis.

In spite of lengthy investigations, the cause of the fire was never determined. Folklore says it was Catherine O'Leary's cow that kicked over a lantern and started the blaze. In fact, Michael Ahern, a reporter for the *Chicago Tribune*, first broadcast that theory in an article the day after the fire. It was no doubt fueled by the anti-Irish sentiment that was prevalent at the time, but it was certainly not true. Ahern finally retracted the story and admitted the fabrication a few decades later, but the O'Leary family lived under a cloud of suspicion for most of their lives.

Many investigators believe that the fire was accidentally started by neighbor Daniel "Peg Leg" Sullivan, who was the first to awaken the O'Learys. Sullivan's mother kept a cow in O'Leary's barn, and perhaps Daniel was bringing feed to the animals when he lit the straw on fire through the careless use of smoking material. Once he realized the extent of the damage, he was undoubtedly fearful of admitting his involvement, so he concocted a tale. His story of spotting the flames from across the street is impossible, because another house next door would have blocked his view. His account of racing for the barn to save the animals is improbable as well. Due to his handicap, he could not run very fast and simply would not have had sufficient time to do as he said. There were many other inconsistencies in his story, but investigators did not pursue the issue.

Another similar theory involves Sullivan but includes a neighbor named Dennis Regan as well. Some researchers believe that Regan attempted to aid Sullivan in rescuing the livestock and extinguishing the fire but aided instead in a coverup when the fire raged out of control. Yet another theory blames a different neighbor, Louis M. Cohn. In his final years, Cohn claimed that he and some neighborhood youths had been playing craps in the barn when they accidentally kicked over a lantern.

Perhaps the most intriguing theory of all is one that would absolve each of those who stood accused. On the same night as the Great Chicago Fire, other devastating fires broke out across the Midwest, including a deadly firestorm in the area of Peshtigo, Wisconsin. The Peshtigo fire remains the worst recorded forest fire in North American history and resulted in about 2,400 deaths. Unfortunately, it was largely ignored by the media of the day, which concentrated instead on the dramatic story of Chicago. Tragic fires also struck in Michigan that night.

According to engineer and physicist Robert Wood, it's possible that the fire began when Biela's Comet created a meteor shower that rained over the Great Lakes area that night. This theory was first proposed and discarded back in 1882, but Wood believes it is not only possible but likely as well. Witnesses at the time mentioned "balls of fire from the sky." Other reports mentioned "blue flames," which could indicate the presence of methane gas, a common element of comets.

Of course, the brutally dry conditions in the Midwest that October set the stage for any happenstance to create a blaze. We will never know the exact cause of the Great Chicago Fire, but we can look back and witness the manner in which it shaped the city's finances, its growth, its culture and even its very geography. Although the legend of the cow and the lantern still lingers, the one unassailable truth is that the fire forever altered the course of a struggling young city.

THE IROQUOIS THEATER FIRE

Is there any living person here? If anyone is alive in here, groan or make a sound.

—*fire marshal surveying the carnage*

In November 1903, Chicago newspapers gushed shamelessly about the new entertainment palace opening in the Loop theater district at 24–28 Randolph Street, between State and Dearborn. It was designed by architect Benjamin Marshall to be not only a thing of beauty but also "absolutely fireproof," a promise that was included in its advertising and stamped across the top of playbills. Marshall boasted that he had studied causes of previous theater fires and had taken all of those factors into consideration as he sketched out plans for the marvelous new venue.

The *Chicago Tribune*'s theater critic, W.L. Hubbard, wrote, "A playhouse so splendid in its every appointment, so beautiful in its every part, so magnificent…The enterprise which made the erection of the new theater possible has given the Chicago playgoers a virtual temple of beauty."

Indeed, the new theater was striking, with a façade of polished granite and Bedford stone that gave the impression of a Roman temple. Inside, lush red velvet and polished mahogany wood greeted guests, who entered through a marble foyer with a spectacular sixty-foot-high ceiling, flanked by white marble staircases ascending to the upper balconies. Gilded mirrors and picture frames hung from the walls, and heavy curtains graced many of the arched doorways.

As the Iroquois was being built during the summer of 1903, a labor strike disrupted the construction for a few weeks. The owners, frantic to get the theater open in time for the popular holiday season, began to cut corners once the workers returned. Some of the key safety features were to be added later, as time permitted. The promised fire alarm system was absent, as were sprinklers and some of the most basic safety devices of the time. One Chicago fire marshal noted that the Iroquois had no fire extinguishers, telephones or water connections; the only firefighting equipment available were a few cans of Kilfyre, a dry chemical used at the time for home stove fires. The nearest fire alarm box was around the corner at Engine Company 13.

Marshall, the architect, also began to make some unwise choices. Despite his grandiose claims of fire safety, he decided that lighted exit signs

On the left is the façade of the Iroquois Theater. This photo was taken while the fire was in progress. Note the dark smoke over the roofline.

detracted from the beauty of the arched doors and did away with them. The "fireproofed" seats were actually stuffed with flammable hemp, a cheap and sturdy upholstery material. A great deal of the interior was furnished with varnished mahogany, another combustible material. The giant stage curtain that was purportedly made of asbestos, in order to protect the theatergoers in case of a backstage fire, was actually a blend of highly combustible cotton velour, wood pulp and asbestos and would be of little value in a fire.

The theater was divided into three seating areas, which would hold a combined total of 1,800 patrons: the main, or "orchestra" floor, which was accessed directly through the grand foyer; the second, "dress circle" level, which could be reached by climbing one of the elegant marble staircases; and the third, "gallery" level, which required a rather confusing course up and down a series of small landings from the dress circle. Ticket prices were, of course, based on the seating area, and the theater management

An unmarked and locked exit door that led to an unfinished fire escape. Many people died as they struggled to escape through this door.

assiduously locked doors between the levels during performances, in order to keep the gallery patrons from sneaking down into the more expensive dress circle or orchestra sections.

The first production at the lavish theater was *Mr. Bluebeard*, a burlesque musical based on the French fairy tale. Popular comedic actor Eddie Foy starred in drag as "Sister Anne," and critics raved about his performance. Although bad weather and labor unrest kept attendance down during the early weeks of its run, people soon began to turn out in droves, filling the house with increasing frequency. The play was considered a "must see," and doting parents across the city made plans to treat their children to a special day at the beautiful new theater.

On Wednesday, December 30, 1903, with school out for the Christmas holidays, the matinee performance was jampacked. The 1,800 seats sold out quickly, but that didn't prevent theater managers from continuing to sell standing room—only tickets. By the time the curtain was raised, the

The massive and elegant theater was advertised as "absolutely fireproof" when it opened just weeks before the tragic fire. The signs in front advertise the musical *Mr. Bluebeard*, which was appearing on that fateful day.

theater was packed with a record-breaking crowd estimated at about 2,000. The standing room area was uncomfortably crowded, filled four deep, and many of those patrons spilled onto the stairs or moved over in front of the exits. The audience that weekday was mostly women and children, and the children rushed excitedly to find the best view.

By all accounts, the show was a smashing success. About 3:15 p.m., in the second act, the ensemble gathered on stage for a dreamy dance scene, "Let Us Swear by the Pale Moonlight." The lights were dimmed, and spotlights emulated a moonlit night. Beautiful ballerinas in blue and gold twirled across the stage as the orchestra played and the chorus sang. Suddenly, in the soft wash of blue and green light, patrons noticed a small flickering tongue of flame high up on one of the stage curtains. At first, many thought it was part of the show, and paid little attention.

The stagehands, however, knew that there was a problem. One of the spotlights had arced and set the curtain on fire, and the flame was now crawling up and licking at the highly flammable oil-painted canvas and

Most of the victims were women and children. Note that the original photograph was blanked out at lower right, probably because it was too gruesome for print. An infant's body can be seen at the bottom of the photo, near the obliterated area.

wood props hanging in the fly gallery above the stage. Someone tried to beat it out with a pole used for pulling props, but that attempt only caused bits of flaming debris to rain down onto the wooden stage. Another stagehand rushed forward with the cans of Kilfyre, but they were woefully inadequate for the task.

By now, the audience realized that this was not part of the show and began to panic as smoke started to fill the auditorium. Eddie Foy was in his dressing room preparing for the next act when he heard the commotion. He ran to make sure that his own small son was safely in the hands of the nanny, and then he rushed out to center stage and spoke to reassure the frightened patrons. He begged them to stay calm and remain in their seats and reminded them that the theater was "absolutely fireproof." As he spoke, a flaming curtain crashed down on the stage, causing the other chorus members to flee in panic, one with her costume afire. Foy quickly instructed conductor Herbert Gillea to "play, play, play, just keep playing!" Gillea led his orchestra in the soothing "Sleeping Beauty" ballet, which momentarily calmed the crowd.

Foy next directed stagehands to lower the fireproof curtain in an effort to protect the audience. In a later interview, he said, "It struck me as I looked out over the crowd during the first act that I had never before seen so many women and children in the audience. Even the gallery was full of mothers and children." As the curtain came down, it snagged on a light reflector that stuck out from under the arch, leaving a twenty-foot gap between the curtain and the wooden stage floor. At this point, Foy's entreaties were having little effect on the panicked crowd, who surged for the exits. Once he realized that he could do no more, Foy himself escaped through a back exit.

Other performers and stagehands tried to flee through the west stage door, which opened inward. It soon jammed due to the crush of trapped people. Amazingly, a passing railroad agent heard the screams and was able to remove the door from its hinges with some tools he carried, allowing them to escape with only minor injuries. Most of the audience, however, was not as lucky.

In the dark and smoky confusion, the lack of exit lighting and heavy curtains across doorways made it difficult to find a way out. Some patrons struggled desperately with "doors" that were actually decorative and

Theater manager Harry J. Powers was charged with involuntary manslaughter due to his role in the disaster, but the charges were later dropped.

not functional. Others found themselves trapped by the heavy iron gates designed to prevent theatergoers from accessing more expensive seats. Some on the upper gallery level made their way to fire escapes, only to find them locked or incomplete. Firefighters found many victims who had fallen to their deaths in the alley behind the theater after climbing out onto the unfinished escapes. Painters working at the Northwestern University building just north of the theater saw what was happening and pushed ladders and boards across the gap to rescue those trapped on a fire platform, and a dozen or so were saved by making the treacherous crawl sixty feet above the ground. Inside the theater, women and children were trampled in the rush, and many died from those injuries before the suffocating smoke even reached them.

At that point, the heavy fire was still mostly contained to the backstage area. A vast number of patrons tried to remain in their seats rather than risk certain death in the crushing, stampeding crowds. They breathed through handkerchiefs and tried to soothe their frightened children, all the while praying for rescue. What they didn't know, however, was that ventilation shafts in the roof, designed to pull hot gases and smoke upward in the event of a fire, were incomplete and wired or nailed shut. When the rear stage doors were opened, cold fresh air from outside rushed in, feeding the flames like a bellows. An enormous fireball exploded under the snagged fire curtain, and in seconds incinerated everything—and everyone—in its path.

At some point, one of the stagehands had run down the street and around the corner to pull a fire alarm. When fire crews first arrived, everything appeared normal from the street, and they wondered if it had been a false alarm. As they attempted to enter the auditorium, however, they found that the doors were hot and would not open. In horror, they realized why the doors were blocked: charred masses of bodies were piled against them, nearly ten feet deep in places. Since the ventilation shafts were not functional and most of the doors were blocked, all the fire and hot gases were trapped inside. Only a few faint wisps of smoke were visible from the rear of the building. Firemen had to use pike poles to peel the bodies apart and shove them aside in order to gain access.

By this time, the fire had nearly burned itself out, and the firemen were able to extinguish it completely in just about ten minutes. The scene that met their eyes, however, would haunt them forever. In addition to the ghastly stench of burned flesh, they found women and children sitting like grotesque statues in the skeletonized seats, petrified in ash. For these poor wretches,

The lavish interior was constructed of white marble and outfitted with deep mahogany and plush velvet.

death had been instantaneous. At each of the exit doors, the trampled and charred bodies of those who fought unsuccessfully to escape the hellish trap lay in a tangle. Outside, scores of injured wandered in shock.

In the finally tally, about 573 people died that day, including 212 children. At least 30 more died later from injuries sustained in the fire, bringing the total to 603 dead. Almost immediately, the city began to look for someone to blame.

The theater owners immediately tried to duck responsibility, in part by a laughable attempt at blaming the manufacturer of Kilfyre for its inadequacy in fighting the conflagration. Many people blamed the mayor, Carter Harrison Jr., for what they perceived to be a terrible lack of oversight on the city's part. A coroner's jury spread the blame far and wide in a scathing indictment that included theater owners, managers and employees; Mayor Harrison; and the Chicago Fire and Building Departments. After years of wrangling in court, no one was held accountable, but a handful of the victims' families received a settlement of $750 for the loss of their loved ones, a sum equal to about $18,000 in today's currency.

The one bit of good to come out of the catastrophe was an immediate improvement in fire codes and enforcement. By the very next day, some theaters in New York had discontinued the practice of selling standing room–only tickets. Mayor Harrison ordered all of Chicago's theaters to be shut

Actor Eddie Foy was considered a hero for his selfless attempts to calm the panicked crowd.

down and inspected, and they weren't allowed to reopen until critical violations were fixed. The public became much more aware of fire safety and no longer accepted vague assurances from greedy operators who told them that premises were "safe" or "fireproof."

Eddie Foy was widely acclaimed as a hero for the calm and authoritative manner in which he attempted to prevent a panic that day, even though his efforts had little effect on the outcome. He went on to develop a vaudeville routine with his children, called "The Seven Little Foys." It was so popular that it was turned into a movie in 1955, starring Bob Hope as Eddie Foy. Eddie died of a heart attack while performing in 1928.

The Iroquois later reopened under the name Colonial Theatre, but it was eventually demolished in 1926. The site now houses the Oriental Theater. The only visible reminder of that horrible day is a small bronze memorial by sculptor Lorado Taft that sits inside the entrance to city hall on LaSalle Street.

THE OUR LADY OF THE ANGELS SCHOOL FIRE

The [95] deaths in this fire are an indictment of those in authority who have failed to recognize their life safety obligations in housing children in structures which are "fire traps."
—*Michele McBride, survivor, in her book* The Fire that Will Not Die

December is a magical time for children. Images of a jolly Santa Claus laden with gifts and toys keep most little girls and boys on their best behavior during the twelfth month, lest they end up on the "naughty list" and find only coal under the tree on December 25. For many Christian children, the month also signifies Advent, a time to go to daily mass, prepare a Nativity scene and celebrate any number of small daily traditions. Most Christian families, in essence, celebrate two December holidays: the birth of Jesus and the arrival of Santa. Of course, the church does its level best to remind the congregants of what it believes is the only true meaning of Christmas, but few families are able to resist the allure of the commercial Christmas as well.

At about 2:30 p.m. on Monday, December 1, 1958, about 1,200 kindergarten through eighth-grade students at Our Lady of the Angels Catholic elementary school on Chicago's near West Side were eagerly awaiting the 3:00 p.m. final bell that would signify the end of the school day. The holiday season was heading into full swing, and the children were restless and filled with anticipation. In only thirty minutes, they would exit their classrooms in an orderly procession, displaying the proper decorum

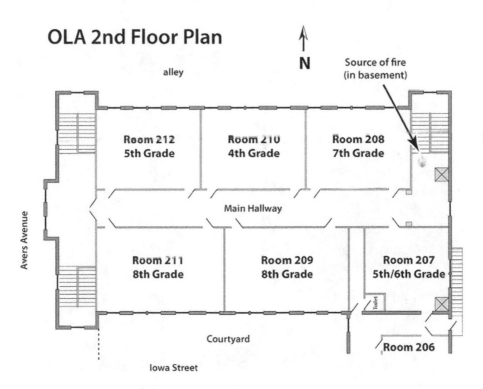

A floor plan of Our Lady of the Angels Catholic school. All of the deaths occurred on the second floor of the north wing. *Illustration by Brian Diskin.*

as required by the nuns. Once they hit the corners, however, out of sisters' views, they would tumble into the street like puppies, racing for home or perhaps stopping for a treat at the candy store across the alley.

The school, at 909 North Avers Avenue, was located in a tightly knit working-class district of mostly Italian, Irish and Polish descent. The vast majority of residents were Catholic, and the church and school formed the heart of the neighborhood. It was a place where children were raised not only by their parents but by the community as well. Virtually every child had an uncle, a grandparent, a cousin or a close neighbor who served as a surrogate parent if mom and dad weren't nearby. Of course, the church was the ultimate authority, one that must be obeyed without question.

On that bitterly cold December day, at about the time that the children were eyeing the clock, James Raymond, the school janitor, was returning to

Firefighters reach ladders to the second-floor classrooms. By this time, most of the remaining children were already dead. The faces of a few living are visible in the second window on the right.

the school from some errands. As he walked through the alley, he spotted smoke curling out from a rear stairwell and an orange glow through a basement window. He rushed into the building to investigate.

Meanwhile, in room 205, a combined fifth- and sixth-grade classroom on the school's second-floor annex, lay teacher Dorothy Coughlan had just sent two students down to the basement boiler room to empty the day's trash. Joseph Brocato and classmate Ronald Eddington, both eleven years old, were finishing up the task when Raymond ran past them, yelling, "Call the fire department!" The janitor ran to the parish house next door and yelled to the housekeeper that the school was on fire and to call the fire department, and then he ran back into the school building through the boiler room. The boys raced back to their classroom, where Ronald whispered urgently into Miss Coughlan's ear. By this time, wisps of smoke had begun to enter the room through the transom over the door. About the same time, Pearl Tristano, the fifth-grade lay teacher in room 206, also noticed the smoke and hurried to room 205 to discuss the matter with Miss Coughlan.

Teachers at the school were strictly forbidden to evacuate without permission from the principal, Sister Mary St. Florence Casey. Coughlan and Tristano rushed to the principal's office, but Sister St. Florence was substitute teaching in room 101 that day, and they couldn't find her. After a quick discussion, the two lay teachers decided to evacuate in defiance of the rules. Their quick thinking saved the lives of all of the students under their care. As they herded the children down the stairs, Miss Tristano pulled the fire alarm, one of only two in the entire school, but it didn't go off. After she had safely deposited her small charges in the church across the street, Tristano ran back to the fire alarm and successfully triggered it on her second attempt.

The first call came into the fire department at 2:42 p.m., from the parish housekeeper. Over the years, there has been some question about the housekeeper's delay in calling in the emergency, since Mr. Raymond was certain that he had arrived on the scene slightly before 2:30 p.m. In the chaos of the disaster, however, few people remembered the events of the day in exactly the same manner. To this day, historical accounts sometimes differ greatly on various points. At any rate, shortly thereafter, a number of emergency calls began to roll in, as visible smoke and flames shot from the rear of the school.

As word of the fire spread, neighborhood men rushed to the scene to rescue the children, arriving before the fire trucks. In fact, the fire department was first directed to the church rectory, around the corner on Iowa Street. By the time they realized their mistake and repositioned the trucks and hoses, precious minutes were lost. In the interim, fathers, grandfathers and passersby struggled to reach the screaming and terrified children trapped on the second floor as thick black smoke and flames shot out around them. The men grabbed ladders from nearby garages and placed them against the building on the alley side, but most were too short to reach the second-floor windows. One group tried lashing two ladders together, but the makeshift device came apart as children started down it, hurtling the tiny victims to the concrete below. Another group of men tried in vain to reach children in classrooms facing the courtyard, but they were stopped by the locked six-foot-tall spiked wrought-iron fence that denied rescuers access. In panic and rage, they tore at the fence with hammers and their bare hands, but it wouldn't budge. Finally, the fire department appeared with sledgehammers and rams, and the lock gave away.

By this time, teachers throughout the school had realized the danger, and most had safely evacuated their classrooms. The devastating exception was the second-floor classrooms of the north wing. The fire had begun in the basement of the rear stairwell in that wing, and thick smoke and superheated gases rapidly spread through the upper-floor hallway. The open stairwell

Neighborhood men tried to rescue trapped children before the fire department arrived, but they were stopped by a locked, six-foot-tall iron gate that blocked access to the courtyard. In addition, the home ladders they had were too short to reach the second-story windows. *Illustration by Brian Diskin.*

acted as a chimney, and as windows shattered at the base from the heat, the influx of fresh oxygen fed the flames and created a mushroom cloud of deadly smoke and fire. Flames crawled into the ceiling through a ventilation grid in the corridor and began to eat away at the roof structure. By the time anyone noticed the smoke seeping into the closed classrooms, it was too late to evacuate through the smoke-filled and suffocating hallways, the only means of escape for most of the rooms. In desperation, some nuns directed students to pile books against the doors in an attempt to slow the incoming smoke. Others instructed children to sit at their desks and pray, in hopes that rescuers would arrive in time.

Room 207, headed by Sister Mary Geraldita Ennis, was at the corner of the building, the only room with access to a fire escape. Nicknamed the "Cheesebox" due to its small size, the crowded room housed both fifth- and sixth-grade students. Unbelievably, the emergency door leading to the escape was locked. A ten-year-old fifth grader named Henry Bertucci crawled through an opened window, grabbed some wires along the side of the building and managed to swing himself onto the fire escape. As he ran down screaming for help, the metal stairs lowered, which allowed janitor Raymond and Father Charles Hund to run up and force open the locked door. Everyone in room 207 escaped, just seconds before the fire flashed over and destroyed everything in its path.

Students in rooms 208 through 212 weren't as lucky. Trapped in the inferno, their only means of escape was through the tall windows two floors above the hard concrete below. Unable to breathe and in agony from the hellish heat at their backs, the children clawed and struggled to reach the windows. Some jumped, landing with a sickening thud in the alleyway as bystanders tried to break their falls. Some deaths and serious injuries were due to falls and not the fire, but many children suffered injuries from both. Others were pushed from the window ledges by children behind them. Still others remained at their desks, clutching rosary beads and praying for a rescue that came too late.

By the time the fire department deployed their long ladders, many of the children were already dead. Firefighters watched in shock as the bright white uniform shirts of the children turned brown from the heat and then burst into flames. One little boy, who had won a small statuette of Jesus in a spelling contest that day, spotted his father in the crowd below. As he stood in the window, he smiled and proudly waved the statuette, until he was pulled

That December was a sad blur of funerals and memorial services.

back into the morass of children struggling at the window. As his anguished father watched in helpless horror, the room flashed over. Survivor Michele McBride (room 209) described watching a classmate burst into flames seconds before she herself fell or was pushed from the window, her body afire. Michele spent several months in hospital burn units and lived out her life with agonizing pain and recurrent medical problems until her untimely death in 2001 from multiple organ failure.

By 2:57 p.m., the fire was declared a 5-11 alarm disaster, and about forty-three fire department vehicles, two hundred firemen and seventy police squadrols responded. Thousands of frantic parents, relatives and neighbors joined the throngs, along with curious bystanders and news reporters and photographers. Television and radio stations interrupted their regular programming to cover the tragedy, and heart-rending images of the fire traveled across the globe. One iconic photo snapped by freelance photographer Steve Lasker depicted fireman Richard Scheidt carrying the lifeless body of John Jajkowski Jr., a fifth-grader in room 212, out of the building. The grief and devastation apparent on firefighter Scheidt's face became symbolic of the disaster, and the photo later served as a fire prevention safety poster nationwide.

Despite its fury, the fire was largely extinguished by 4:30 p.m., but the search for victims and survivors was only beginning. Children who were able to escape without severe injuries were scattered throughout the neighborhood; some ran for home, some sought shelter with neighbors or friends and others hunkered down in the church across the street. One little girl, bloodied, burned and wandering in shock, was scooped up by a stranger and rushed to a nearby hospital. The weather that day was bitterly cold, and most of the children had escaped without

A monument at Queen of Heaven Cemetery in suburban Hillside pays tribute to the lost children.

coats or had lost their shoes in their desperate scramble for survival. Shock and trauma dimmed the odds for the most severely injured, who quickly overwhelmed the area hospitals.

Late into the night, parents searched in a nightmarish quest to find their children, not knowing if they would find them at a hospital or in a morgue. Some of the victims were burned well beyond recognition and could only be identified through dental records. Firefighters told gruesome tales of attempting to remove bodies from the devastation, only to have them crumble apart as they were lifted. The horror of that day remained seared in the memory of those who lived it, as well as in the city that witnessed it.

In the final tally, ninety-two children and three nuns died in the conflagration. A total of eighty-seven children perished on the scene, but five more succumbed to their injuries at a later date. One boy, William Edington, fought to survive until August 1959, when he finally lost his battle. Hundreds of others were injured, some with critical burns that haunted them for life. That Christmas season was a devastating string of funerals and memorial services, as well as unopened presents under the tree that parents couldn't bear to look at. After the fire, many families moved away, unable to deal with the constant reminders of the tragedy.

Although the cause of the fire was never officially named, all signs point to the conclusion that it was arson. A ten-year-old boy in room 206 had been excused to go to the bathroom at 2:00 p.m., about the time the fire likely started. Fire investigators found a burned pack of matches near a cardboard trash barrel at the base of the stairway, which was determined to be the source of the fire. A few years later, the same boy was connected to a string of arsons in his new neighborhood in Cicero. While being questioned about those small fires, he confessed to setting the Our Lady of the Angels fire but later recanted. In his confession, however, the boy related details that only the arsonist would have known. The judge in the inquiry and the Catholic Archdiocese were loath to prosecute a child, believing that it would be a "death sentence" for the youngster. In reality, it also could have greatly increased the church's liability had the fire been purposefully set, a factor that likely influenced their beneficence. The suspected arsonist died in 2004 and was never charged with the crime.

Investigators instead focused on factors that made the fire so lethal. The school was built in stages between 1910 and 1951. Although the exterior was brick, almost the entire interior was highly varnished wood, with linoleum flooring and highly flammable acoustical ceiling tiles. There were only two fire alarms in the entire building, both on the first floor, and the alarms were not hooked up to the fire department. The staircase was not fireproofed, and fire doors, where they existed, were largely left open. In 1949, the city of Chicago adopted a new municipal fire code that required sprinklers and many other lifesaving upgrades, but the school was "grandfathered" in and not required to comply, since it had been built before the new codes were adopted. (The small annex, built in 1951, did incorporate some upgrades, but not enough to significantly affect the outcome.)

In the end, the National Fire Protection Association (NFPA) blamed the massive casualties on a lack of sufficient exits. Once the hallway became impassable, the students in rooms 208 through 212 had no other means of escape. Fire Commissioner R.J. Quinn of Chicago disagreed with the NFPA's conclusion and believed that the loss of life was caused by a delayed alarm to the fire department. In truth, the disaster encompassed a "perfect storm" of small failures and misjudgments, and there is no shortage of blame to be shouldered by the Chicago Archdiocese, the Chicago Fire Commission and the complacency of those who allowed profit and convenience to supersede the lives of ninety-two of Chicago's littlest angels.

Part II
DEPTHS OF DISASTER

THE GREAT CHICAGO FLOOD OF 1992

[F]ish are swimming in the basement of the [Merchandise] *Mart...I think someone should wake up the mayor!*

—*WMAQ reporter Larry Langford*

Chicago is a city surrounded by water. Perched precariously on the southwestern edge of Lake Michigan, the city's downtown (aka "the Loop") looks out over a vast expanse of deep blue water that stretches far beyond what the human eye can perceive, more than one hundred miles to the distant shores of Michigan. Flowing inward from the lake is the Chicago River and its various forks and tributaries. Unlike normal rivers that flow *into* larger bodies of water, the Chicago River was engineered in the early 1900s to flow backward *away* from the lake through a series of locks, in order to keep the lakefront water clean and free of sewage. The river winds throughout downtown like a tenacious, weedy vine, creating islands of tall buildings that seem to sprout directly from the watery depths. In fact, large portions of the lakefront were once submerged but were claimed as land by architects, engineers and alchemists, who stubbornly fought back the waters with landfill and concrete, raising glass and steel monoliths from the mud.

In spite of its proximity, water has rarely created much of a problem for the downtown area. Rain and swollen streams are quickly swallowed by the mighty lake or, to the dismay of homeowners, channeled to suburban basements unlucky enough to be too far removed from nature's giant reservoir. Locks and dams and breakwaters create the illusion of control, and usually the system works fairly well. Water is a tricky foe, however, and has a way of demanding respect when complacency sets in.

In September 1991, a crew from Great Lakes Dredge and Dock Company was doing some rehabilitation work below the Kinzie Street Bridge on the North Branch of the Chicago River. Working from a barge, they were replacing some of the wooden pilings on the southeast side of the bridge. These groupings of pilings, known as "dolphins," are used to moor boats and protect bridge abutments from boat collisions. As they removed old dolphins, water and mud flowed in to fill the old holes. The crew then used heavy equipment to drive the new pilings down through the water, silt and mud to anchor them firmly into the solid ground beneath the river, about three feet south of their original locations. Unbeknownst to the crew, however, was the fact that there was precious little solid ground underneath that particular section of the river. Instead, close below the muddy river bottom was a decaying and mostly deserted freight tunnel from the early twentieth century. Although the pilings didn't pierce the tunnel's roof, they

The Kinzie Street Bridge across the Chicago River. Workers driving wooden pilings near the bridge abutment damaged the roof of an underground tunnel, allowing the entire downtown area to flood. *Photo by Jeremy Atherton.*

weakened it substantially and set the stage for what would later become one of the costliest disasters in Chicago's history.

The tunnel under Kinzie Street composes just a small section of the sixty-two miles of abandoned miniature freight tracks that riddle Chicago's underground. The tunnels were established in 1899, when workers started to excavate through the basement of a tavern near LaSalle and Madison Streets. They dug through the heavy clay by hand and by knife, removing the debris through the tavern at night. Most of the work was done surreptitiously because there was never a formal review of property rights or official sanction for the project. The original intent was to create a space to house telephone cables, but soon the Illinois Tunnel Company quietly began to install two-foot-gauge railroad tracks to move freight and mail and deliver coal to building subbasements along the route. In 1912, the company was reorganized as the Chicago Tunnel Company, and the mini freight business boomed.

By its peak in the 1930s, the Chicago Tunnel Company was running about 3,000 freight cars and 150 locomotives deep beneath Chicago streets. Unfortunately, Chicago's new subway transit system shared the tunnels' subterranean turf and wiped out sections of the most profitable routes in favor of the new passenger trains. Competition from surface motor trucks and conversion from coal heat to gas also hurt, and by 1959 the company had gone bankrupt and had simply abandoned the tunnels. Scavengers and scrappers removed most of the train cars and copper wiring, as well as anything else of value that they could salvage.

For decades, the tunnel system languished in legal limbo, with no clear ownership or regular maintenance. Eventually, Commonwealth Edison and various other utility companies began to ask the city for permission to use the space for cable vaults—ironically, the purpose for which it was originally designed. Few Chicagoans, however, knew or cared much about the silent and dark warren of passageways beneath their feet. That is, until the trouble began.

In January 1992, some cable television employees were inspecting their equipment lines in the tunnel near the Kinzie Street Bridge when they noticed a breach in the ceiling oozing mud and water. They immediately videotaped the scene and contacted city hall with the urgent news. In its usual sloth-like bureaucratic crawl, the city began the laborious process of acquiring bids to seal the leak. Months later, nothing had been done to patch the deteriorating spot because all of the initial bids exceeded the city's estimate of $10,000 for the repair. Instead of reevaluating the estimate, acting Department of Transportation commissioner John LaPlante simply put out a call for more bids. By now, more than three months had passed since the day cable employees had raced their urgent observations to the powers that be in city government.

On Monday, April 13, 1992, shortly before 6:00 a.m., a building engineer at Chicago's Merchandise Mart discovered flooding in the massive building's third subbasement. Unable to determine the source, he dialed 911 to notify the city's emergency services. Within minutes, the Chicago Fire Department and city public works employees responded in force, but they could not figure out where the water was coming from. While they pondered this unlikely predicament, more calls started to roll into 911. Soon, it was apparent that the Merchandise Mart wasn't alone in its troubles.

The venerable Marshall Field's State Street flagship store reported flooding in two of its subbasements, with water levels reaching forty feet deep. Rival Carson Pirie Scott wasn't faring much better, nor were any of the other neighboring buildings on State Street. By the time employees began to appear at downtown offices to begin their workweek, the scope of the disaster was just becoming apparent. Water seemed to be pouring in from everywhere. Subway lines along State and Dearborn had to be evacuated and closed as they began to fill. In desperation, city workers started closing

The Illinois Tunnel Company ran freight and mail trains through subterranean tunnels under Chicago's Loop.

water mains, including a massive forty-two-inch main pipe under LaSalle Street, but still the waters rose.

The financial district along LaSalle was forced to shut down as water began to bubble up in basements along that street. The Chicago Mercantile Exchange's closing affected worldwide grain futures trading, which resulted in an estimated loss of $25 billion in trade due to the disaster. One pending trade of fifty-four thousand tons of soybeans to Taiwan was delayed, causing instability in the world market for weeks to come. Government offices and private businesses alike raced to save irreplaceable records that were all too often stored in basement vaults. Retailers such as Field's and Carson's lost valuable inventory and were forced to temporarily lay off employees as a direct result of the flood. More than one hundred buildings were ultimately damaged, some housing dozens of different tenants who each suffered their own losses.

As underground utilities vaults flooded and began to short out, the fire department crews were left with no choice but to shut off power to most of the Loop and begin the arduous task of evacuating the heart of the third-most-populous city in the United States. Darkened buildings, stalled public transit systems and scrambled telecommunications all added to the chaos. It was a surreal scene as stranded commuters, unable to enter their workplaces or return home via the subway, milled about in confusion. Above ground there were no signs of any sort of disaster; it was just a typical early spring day in the city—except, of course, for the harried scrambling of emergency personnel as they tried to cope with a strange subterranean drama playing out far below the feet of Chicago's pedestrians.

While city workers struggled to determine the source of the onslaught, a WMAQ radio overnight crime reporter named Larry Langford was listening intently to his police scanner. He noticed that building engineers at the Merchandise Mart had reported seeing fish in the floodwater. He immediately reached the common-sense conclusion that the appearance of fish ruled out the possibility of it being a water main break, a fact that had apparently escaped the first responders. Larry jumped into his car and headed for the Mart, which is situated on the riverfront and bordered by Orleans, Wells and Kinzie Streets. When he arrived on the scene and looked down at the river, he immediately spotted an ominous clue right next to the Kinzie Street Bridge: a large, debris-filled spinning swirl of water, which he described as looking like "a giant drain." He reported this astute observation on the air, and the riverfront was soon swarming with a small army of fire, police and city personnel.

Sure enough, the giant water swirl was indeed the source of Chicago's woes. A hole the size of an automobile had opened in the roof of the underground tunnel, and now the waters of the Chicago River (and some of its finned residents) were pouring unabated into the ancient freight system and on into building basements and the subway. Now that the problem had been identified, fixing it was the next challenge.

To make the repair work easier, the city closed the river locks at Lake Michigan and opened locks downstream, thus lowering the river and reducing the flow. Workers first tried to plug the hole in the riverbed from above by dumping in cement and gravel, but after sixty-five truckloads the water hadn't slowed its course. In desperation, they began tossing in more creative leak stoppers such as old mattresses and other types of fill, but nothing seemed to exhaust the endless drain. Finally, a private company called Kenny Construction came up with a better solution: it drilled perpendicular shafts down into the flooded tunnel on each side of the breach and placed emergency plugs to seal off the damaged area. Once they had successfully stemmed new flow, the problem of draining away the existing floodwater still remained.

Luckily, Chicago loves tunnels and was in the process of building new ones capable of draining the old ones. The Metropolitan Water Reclamation District of Greater Chicago's $4 billion Tunnel and Reservoir Plan (TARP), known locally as "Deep Tunnel," is an ongoing project designed to control

A freight train in the tunnel near Marshall Field & Company's subbasement.

flooding and water pollution throughout the Chicagoland area. It is an arrangement of huge tunnels bored through limestone bedrock at a depth up to three hundred feet below the surface. These tunnels collect sewage and storm water from overflowing municipal systems and feed it into massive reservoirs, where it can be treated and slowly discharged. The project began in 1972 and is not scheduled for completion until about 2029, but by 1992 a section of the system was functional. City workers were able to drain water from the old freight tunnels into the "Deep Tunnel" system and finally allow downtown businesses to begin the arduous task of cleanup.

The great flood cost the city an estimated $1.5 billion. Loop businesses remained closed for at least three days, but some took weeks to reopen. All downtown parking was suspended, and many of the subways had to be rerouted or closed during cleanup. Above ground, streets were filled with tangles of hoses and sump pumps, while fans and dehumidifiers struggled to dry out the soggy and musty building interiors. Many businesses held "flood sales," definitely a new marketing concept for the city. Since the disaster occurred right before tax day, the IRS granted a temporary disaster extension to those affected.

As insurance companies began to look at their losses, an interesting twist developed. Insurance companies generally do not cover flood damage, but they do cover damage caused by leaks or sewer backups. For years, ensuing court battles struggled to define the cause of the disaster, as the insurers tried to insist that it was a flood—and therefore not covered. In the end, the courts ruled that it was a massive leak, and the companies had to pony up and pay the claims. In the vernacular of Chicago, however, it will always be the "Great Chicago Flood"—somehow, the "Great Leak" just doesn't have the same ring to it.

THE TRAGEDY OF THE SS *EASTLAND*

As I watched in disoriented stupefaction, a steamer large as an ocean liner slowly turned over on its side [in the river] *as though it were a whale going to take a nap...I thought I had gone crazy.*

—*Jack Woodford, witness*

Saturday, July 24, 1915, was a day filled with excitement and anticipation for workers at the massive Western Electric Hawthorne Works plant in suburban

Cicero. The company's annual outing was scheduled for that day, and this year employees and their families could enjoy a lake cruise to Michigan City, Indiana, for a day of picnicking and other festivities. The company had chartered six Great Lakes passenger steamers for the occasion and handed out more than seven thousand adult tickets; children were to be admitted free. Eager workers arose early and dressed in their summer finery for what promised to be a memorable day of sun and fun.

Western Electric Company was the manufacturing and electrical engineering arm of American Bell Telephone, the predecessor to AT&T. In 1915, nearly twenty-five thousand employees worked out of the Hawthorne plant, many of them Polish and Czech immigrants. The five-million-square-foot facility was so massive that it boasted its own railroad, and workers routinely had to ride bicycles to get from one end of the complex to the other. The company claimed that it manufactured forty-three thousand varieties of telephone apparatus, and it was responsible for such important breakthroughs as the high-vacuum tube, the condenser microphone and air-to-ground communications. Later, the Western Electric engineers would develop groundbreaking radar systems.

On that sunny July morning, however, work was not on the minds of the employees. Thousands of them lined up on the docks of the Chicago River, waiting impatiently to board the ships. The *Theodore Roosevelt*, the *Petoskey*, the

The SS *Eastland* was a Great Lakes passenger steamer that ran between Chicago and the Indiana-Michigan shoreline.

Maywood, the *Racine*, the *Rochester* and the *Eastland* all stood at ready to handle the crowds. The tickets didn't assign passengers to any particular ship; they could board at will. The *Eastland* and the *Theodore Roosevelt* were the newest and the most luxurious, however, and were scheduled to be the first to leave, so it seemed that everyone jostled to board one of those two.

The *Eastland* was built in 1902 by the Jenks Ship Building Company, under commission by the Michigan Steamship Company. Almost immediately, the ship proved to have design problems. Its center of gravity was fixed too high, rendering it unstable and top-heavy. On two occasions, it developed a dangerous list while filled with passengers, and the crew had to quickly redistribute passengers and take on ballast to remedy the situation. In one instance, it listed so badly that water flowed past its gangplanks before the crew was able to right it.

The Eastland Navigation Company, which owned the ship from 1909 to 1914, was so concerned about the boat's reputation that it placed a half-page ad in the *Cleveland Plain Dealer* challenging anyone who could prove the steamer unsafe to come forward:

> [T]*here are thousands of people who know absolutely nothing about boats, the rules and regulations for their running, and inspection and licensing*

The *Eastland* was often used for private excursions. This card advertised the Diebold Safe & Lock Company's cruise to Cedar Point, Indiana.

of the same by the U.S. Government. In the hope of influencing this class of people there have been put into circulation stories to the effect that the Steamer Eastland is not safe...[a $5,000 reward is offered] *to anyone who can...bring forth a naval engineer, a marine architect, a shipbuilder, or any one qualified to pass on the merits of a ship who will say that the Steamer Eastland is not a seaworthy ship, or that she would not ride out any storm or weather any condition that can arise on either lake or ocean.*

Of course, no one answered the challenge, and the *Eastland* continued to ply the waves of Lake Michigan. However, its licensed capacity was reduced several times in light of its propensity to list: first from 3,300 to 2,800 and then once more to 2,400. Eventually, it was only licensed to carry 1,125 passengers. The owners protested, and just three weeks before the picnic, Inspector Robert Reid granted an amended certificate that allowed the *Eastland* to carry 2,500 passengers.

In retrospect, it was a poor decision. New maritime rules enacted after the loss of life on the RMS *Titanic* required all passenger ships to carry enough lifeboats to rescue everyone on board, since many of the *Titanic*'s victims could have been saved if there had been sufficient lifeboats. The new laws

The *Eastland* on its side in the river. Many passengers on the upper starboard decks were able to clamber onto the hull as the ship slowly rolled, but those on the port side were pitched into the water or trapped below decks.

were intended to prevent a repeat disaster. For the *Eastland*, this retrofitting added three lifeboats and six large life rafts (ten tons total) to the top deck. In addition, the owners had recently added cement flooring to the main and 'tween decks to replace rotted wooden planking. This added another fifty-seven tons to the already top-heavy ship.

To make matters worse, the ship had taken on a full load of coal the night before in anticipation of its trip. It was estimated that it ended up with 104 tons aboard, 79 tons to port and only 24 tons to starboard. The next morning's boarding was planned for the starboard side, so perhaps the uneven distribution of coal was intentional and meant to balance the weight of incoming passengers. If so, it didn't work.

At 6:30 a.m., the Western Electric employees who scrambled aboard the ship as it was docked just west of the Clark Street Bridge had no knowledge of these destabilizing changes or of the fact that the crew had emptied the ballast tanks in an effort to take on more passengers. As they happily piled on board, the ship began to list about ten degrees to starboard. Because many people were concentrated on the upper starboard deck, waving to friends on the dock, the slight list made sense. In an effort to correct it, the crew added water to the port ballast tanks. No one in authority was paying much attention to how many people actually boarded; some estimate that at least 3,200 were on the ship at the time of the accident.

Although the crew didn't yet seem to realize it, the ship was in grave danger. It was grossly overloaded with passengers, many of whom were still above deck. At this point, the center of gravity was now above the center of buoyancy, a condition known as "negative metacentric height." Some crew members began to urge people below deck in an effort to increase stability. By 6:53 a.m., the ship began a ten-degree list to port. The crew added more water to the ballast tanks. At first, the list increased, but by 7:18 a.m. the ship seemed to right itself.

By this time, other boat captains and some knowledgeable bystanders tried to warn the *Eastland*'s captain, Harry Pedersen, that his ship was in danger, but he paid no attention. Shortly after 7:20 a.m., the gangplank was raised, and the crew cast off the stern (rear) lines to begin the voyage. Almost immediately, the ship began to sway and rock in the water. At first, the passengers weren't frightened and even joked about the motion. Soon, however, the port list became so severe that water began to pour in through portholes. The passengers tried to scramble to the starboard side, but now dishes, furniture and even a piano began to slide and crash across the deck.

The tug *Kenosha* wedged itself between the wharf and the *Eastland*'s hull, serving as a floating walkway for survivors. Its crew also rescued people from the water.

At about 7:28 a.m., the *Eastland*, its bow still moored to the wharf, gently rolled onto its side without a splash and settled into the muddy river bottom. Although the water was only about twenty feet deep and the boat was literally still tied to the dock, the passengers below decks were immediately trapped in a watery grave. Those above deck were tossed into the water and struggled to stay afloat. The Chicago River through downtown is uniformly deep, with nearly vertical banks; swimmers couldn't simply wade to shore. Their only hope was to be pulled out or to clamber onto pilings or other structures in the water. Some of the passengers on the starboard deck had instinctively climbed over the railing as the boat rolled, and now they found themselves standing on the hull of the steamer.

Due to the number of witnesses, help was immediate. In fact, the first calls to police and fire came in while the ship was still upright, from observers who realized that it was doomed. The tug *Kenosha* was immediately wedged between the wharf and the capsized ship, serving as a floating bridge for those who managed to scramble onto the *Eastland*'s hull. Its crew also pulled people from the water. Other ships in the vicinity threw life preservers and lines to those struggling in the murky river. Employees of a nearby warehouse tossed down wooden egg crates and other pieces of wood to serve as flotation aids.

Rescuers cut holes in the hull in an attempt to rescue survivors. By the time they reached them, most had drowned.

Although it didn't take long to gather victims—both dead and alive—from the water, rescuers realized that some people were still alive and imprisoned within the sunken steamer. Onlookers could hear the faint screams and shouts from inside the ship, as the trapped passengers pounded helplessly on the hull. Emergency workers began the tortuous chore of cutting through the thick steel to reach those trapped inside. By the time they reached them, many more had drowned, and only a few survivors were lifted from within the hull.

Once it was clear that all of the living were saved, rescuers turned to the grim job of recovery and identification. In spite of the heroic response from onlookers, about 844 people died in the disaster. Some accounts place the number even higher, but the "official" death toll was set at 844: 841 passengers, 2 crew members from the *Eastland* and 1 crew member from the *Petoskey* who died in the rescue effort. Many of the victims were young single women who worked at the plant or children from the families who had joined the excursion. The city morgue could not handle even a small percentage of the bodies, so a temporary morgue was established at the Second Regiment Armory on Sangamon Street. For days, there was a grim procession of mourners as families and friends came to claim their dead. Some weren't claimed for several days because there was no one left alive to claim them—in fact, twenty-two entire families were wiped out in the disaster.

Western Electric closed the Hawthorne Plant for most of the week to allow the remaining employees time to grieve and attend services for their friends and coworkers. In a surprising show of corporate sensitivity, the company also waited about a month before they began the task of replacing the dead workers. Many of the survivors remained with the company after the tragedy, including one young woman who worked there for almost another forty years, until her retirement in the early 1950s.

The *Eastland* itself also survived the disaster. Within three weeks of the sinking, work crews righted and refloated the ship, which was then sold to the Illinois Naval Reserve and renamed the USS *Wilmette*. Its upper decks were removed, and with a total load of naval personnel never exceeding 375, the ship performed quite well. In 1918, it was converted to a gunboat for use during World War I, but the war ended before it saw any action. The *Wilmette* spent most of its life as a training vessel, until it was finally decommissioned and sold for scrap in 1946.

Most of the dead were placed in a temporary morgue at the Second Regiment Armory building. The building now houses Oprah Winfrey's Harpo Studios, and it is reputedly haunted.

Three weeks after capsizing at its dock, the *Eastland* was lifted from the mud by the tug *Favorite*, with help from a floating crane.

After the accident, criminal and civil suits were quickly filed against the ship's owners and crew, but little came of it. Part of the problem was that the charges that were originally fixed against the defendants—criminal negligence and manslaughter—were reduced by the judge to "conspiracy to operate an unsafe ship." Although greed and stupidity might have played a large part, there was obviously no organized conspiracy, and they were found not guilty. The civil suit dragged on for nearly twenty years. Eventually, the judge ruled in favor of the plaintiffs, but it was a hollow victory. The award was limited to the salvage value of the *Eastland*'s hull, which was valued at about $50,000. Out of that, the court agreed to pay the costs associated with salvaging the ship and some legal costs. In the end, the victims' families came away empty-handed.

In an odd twist, Oprah Winfrey's Harpo Studios now occupies the renovated old armory, and employees of Harpo tell of frequent supernatural encounters. They often hear the sound of children's laughter and sometimes see a ghostly apparition, which they have dubbed "the Gray Lady." Coincidence perhaps, but its connection to the disaster creates an eerie link between the studio and the haunting memories from so long ago.

THE SINKING OF THE *LADY ELGIN*

O! Them death screams! Nobody knows what it was except those that were there!

—Jacob Cook, survivor

I would call it the Titanic *of the Great Lakes.*
—maritime historian Brendon Baillod

September 1860 was a turbulent time in the United States. Divided by the issue of slavery, Union states in the North and Confederate states in the South were engaged in a bitter dispute that would soon lead to the Civil War. Even within states, angry rhetoric separated residents into opposing camps, while lawmakers struggled to find equilibrium.

Nowhere was the rift more apparent than in Milwaukee, Wisconsin. Governor Alexander Randall was an ardent abolitionist and outspoken opponent of the Fugitive Slave Act of 1850, which required law enforcement officers to arrest and return any suspected slaves to their masters. The act also created fines and jail sentences for citizens accused of aiding or harboring slaves. Randall believed that if abolitionist candidate Abraham Lincoln did not win the upcoming election, Wisconsin's only recourse would be to secede from the Union and declare war against the federal government. In preparation for the possibility, he began to survey the state's various militias to see if they would support his plan. Commander Garrett Barry of Milwaukee's Irish Third Ward Union Guard responded that while he abhorred slavery and was himself an abolitionist, he would not take up arms against the U.S. government, which he considered treason.

Randall was enraged by Barry's response and accused him of disloyalty to the state. He ordered the unit to disband and seized all of their weapons, cutting off all state support. Barry refused to back down and sought to rearm his unit as an independent militia. For that, he would need funding. With help from local political groups, Barry chartered the *Lady Elgin*, a wooden-hulled side-wheel steamship, for a cruise to Chicago to attend a rally and hear presidential candidate Stephen A. Douglas give a speech. It would be an opportunity to create awareness of their plight and do some fundraising. The Guard was joined by members of two German light infantry divisions,

The *Lady Elgin* at dock. The side-wheel steamer was considered a safe and reliable passenger ship.

the Green Jaegers and the Black Jaegers, as well as the Milwaukee City Band and many other prominent members of the community.

The *Lady Elgin* departed Milwaukee from the Dooley, Martin and Dousman Company dock late in the evening of Thursday, September 6, 1860, headed to Chicago. The trip down the lake was uneventful, and excursionists enjoyed a busy Friday in the Windy City, attending a rally, participating in a parade and listening to political speeches. As the time neared for the return trip to Milwaukee on Friday night, however, the weather turned ominous.

At the time, many passenger lines operated in a rather casual and opportunistic manner, and passenger manifests either didn't exist or were sloppy and incomplete. If the *Lady Elgin* kept a manifest, it went down with the ship. No one knows for certain how many voyagers piled aboard for the return trip to Milwaukee that night, but best estimates are between five hundred and seven hundred people, along with about fifty head of cattle in the hull used for ballast. In addition to the original passengers, many new ones had joined the ship in Chicago, some un-ticketed and perhaps unintentional, but they were swept along in the festivities and neglected to disembark before departure. Captain Jack Wilson, an experienced Great Lakes skipper, was

The schooner *Augusta* at dock in Chicago after collision. Note the crew clustered at the bow, examining the damage.

concerned about the weather and inclined to delay the departure, but the travelers were tired and restless and wanted to return home. And so, against his better judgment, Captain Wilson steered away from the Chicago dock at about 11:30 p.m., out into the face of an approaching gale.

Despite the vicious wind and waves, the passengers were dancing to the brass band and having a wonderful time. The *Lady Elgin* was a sturdy ship, and it plowed stubbornly through the rain and fog, its lights glowing like a beacon in the night. Its progress was very slow, however, as it struggled to make headway in winds in excess of fifty- to sixty-mile-per-hour. By 2:30 a.m., the ship was just north of Chicago, about ten miles off the coast of Winnetka, Illinois. Suddenly, a shadowy attacker loomed out of the darkness and headed straight for the *Lady Elgin*'s port flank.

The *Augusta*, a 129-foot, 266-ton, two-masted schooner was headed to Chicago with a load of lumber when the gale hit. Under almost full sail, its load had shifted and it was nearly on its side, racing through the water and out of control as its crew struggled to right it. Seconds later, the schooner slammed into the passenger ship with a sickening thud, burying its bowsprit just aft of the *Lady Elgin*'s port paddle wheel. The forward momentum of the side-wheeler caused the *Augusta* to swing around, and for a few agonizing

The collision happened at night in fog, rain and gale-force winds. The ships immediately drifted apart and lost sight of each other. Only the *Augusta* survived.

moments the *Lady Elgin* dragged the schooner through the dark as both crews struggled to determine what had happened. Soon the *Augusta* pulled loose, and the ships were quickly separated in the wind and waves. The *Augusta* crew thought that they had suffered the worst of the damage and watched in anger as the side-wheeler steamed on through the night. The *Augusta's* skipper, Captain Darius Malott, observed: "That steamer sure got away from here in a hurry!" Although the schooner's bow was crushed, it was still water-tight, and the crew raced on for Chicago, fearing that they might founder in the waves.

As the *Augusta* slipped away, Captain Wilson rushed to assess the damage to his ship. He had been asleep below deck when the collision occurred, but the jarring crash jolted him from his slumber. When he reached the engine room, he knew immediately that the *Lady Elgin* was doomed. The *Augusta* had opened a gaping wound in its victim's side, and water was pouring in from a gash below the waterline. While First Mate George Davis ran to the pilothouse and ordered the ship to steam full speed for shore, Wilson struggled to lighten the ship in hopes of raising the damaged area above the water and buying some time. The cattle penned below decks were driven overboard amid a stampede of hooves and panicked braying. The crew began to toss cargo from the hold and moved a shipment of iron stoves to the starboard side in an attempt to cause an intentional list and lift the damaged port side.

Despite the gallant efforts, the *Lady Elgin* began to break apart in the waves. One lifeboat was lowered, but in the pandemonium the crew neglected to tether it to the ship or even grab oars, and it drifted away helplessly with just First Mate Davis and a few other crew members on board. The breach in the hull split the ship nearly in two, cutting off the passengers' access to most of the life preservers. Captain Wilson and others began tearing off pieces of decking, doors and anything else that would float and tossing them into the water to use as flotation aids. The mortally wounded ship sank quickly by the stern, and about twenty minutes after the initial collision only a small section of the bow and a few sizable sections of decking remained afloat. In the water, an estimated five hundred survivors struggled in the waves, clinging to whatever debris they were able to grasp.

Despite frequent comparisons to the *Titanic*, there were a few major differences in the two shipwrecks. The *Titanic* sank on a clear, dead-calm, starlit night, but those unfortunates who landed in the freezing water quickly succumbed to fatal hypothermia. In contrast, Lake Michigan's water was

Rescuers on land struggled heroically to save those being dashed to death on the rocks from the violent surf.

warm enough that September night, but crashing waves, howling winds and driving rain made it difficult if not impossible for the survivors to remain afloat. Jagged streaks of lightning provided the only illumination to the scene, as the human flotilla drifted toward the far-off shore.

As dawn broke, the lifeboat carrying First Mate Davis finally reached shore near the high bluffs of Winnetka. An exhausted Davis somehow scrambled up the sheer bluff to the first house in sight, that of the Gage family. Mr. J. Gage quickly awakened his neighbors, and the men grabbed ropes and ladders and hurried to offer what assistance they could. Someone from the household also ran to the Chicago & Milwaukee railroad station and sent a telegraph about the emergency to Chicago. By 8:00 a.m., the shores were lined with bystanders and would-be rescuers, who were largely forced to watch helplessly as the furiously crashing surf and brutal undertow dashed survivors to their deaths on the jagged rocks, just a few precious yards from safety.

Several students from nearby Northwestern University also rushed to the scene. One of them, Edward W. Spencer, had grown up on the banks of the Mississippi River and was an avid swimmer. With a rope tied around his waist and held by helpers onshore, Spencer dove fearlessly into the roiling water and swam out to the survivors. One by one, he dragged them back safely to shore, where other rescuers carried them to a warming fire and wrapped them in blankets. As he swam for one drowning man, a piece of decking tossed by the waves smashed him in the face, causing profuse bleeding. His friends, believing that he was seriously injured, began to pull the rope to bring him back to shore. Spencer, however, refused to abort his rescue attempt. He pulled off the rope and tossed it aside and successfully rescued another victim. He spent more than six hours in the raging breakers that day and rescued eighteen people before he collapsed in delirium. The physical and emotional toll of his heroism was so severe that Spencer was an invalid for quite a while afterward and had to abandon his studies. On his sickbed, he repeatedly asked his brother Will, also a student at Northwestern, "Will, did I do my full duty—did I do my best?" Northwestern University still displays a plaque and a picture of Spencer, "the hero of the *Lady Elgin*."

Although as many as 400 survivors reached shallow waters that morning, only about 160 were saved—some accounts say fewer than 100. About 60 people were rescued by a tugboat offshore, while others eventually fought their way to safety or were saved by people onshore. The vast majority,

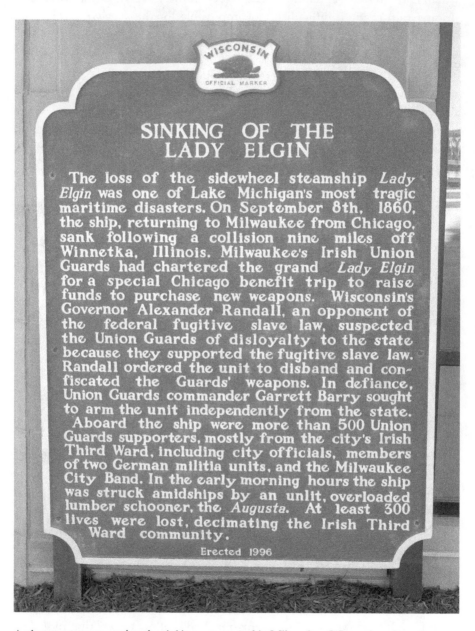

A plaque commemorating the sinking was erected in Milwaukee, Wisconsin, where the excursion originated.

however, perished in sight of shore, pummeled by the furious waves. Captain Wilson, who had shepherded about 100 passengers through the night on a large raft of decking, was smashed to his death on the rocks when he left the raft to rescue two women who had slipped away in exhaustion. His body came ashore three days later on the opposite side of the lake, at Michigan City, Indiana, a distance of more than sixty miles. Commander Barry also died while attempting a rescue. Debris and bodies continued to wash ashore for months, a grim reminder of that horrible night.

When the *Augusta* eventually limped into port at Chicago, leaking badly and with a crushed bow, news of the disaster had already reached the city. The ship was met with an angry crowd threatening to lynch the captain and crew and burn the ship. Captain Malott was stunned, believing that the *Lady Elgin* had steamed away unhurt from a glancing blow. Most reports of the day were incredibly harsh on the *Augusta* and its crew, but in reality there was little assistance they could have offered due to the nature of the storm and the *Augusta*'s own damage and instability. In any case, Malott was arrested and held for formal hearings. The newspapers of the day even suggested that Malott was a Confederate agent and that the ramming was intentional to destroy the Union Guard.

Eventually, Malott was released and found work with his crew on another ship, the *Mojave*. The *Augusta* was renamed the *Colonel Cook* and was quietly moved to service on the Atlantic coast. Four years later, almost on the anniversary of the *Lady Elgin*'s sinking, the *Mojave* and all aboard disappeared without a trace. Most people assumed that it had foundered in a remote area of northern Lake Michigan, but whispered rumors were that "justice was served," indicating that the captain and crew might have been lynched in retaliation.

The sinking of the *Lady Elgin* nearly wiped out Milwaukee's Irish Third Ward, where almost every family had a loved one, friend or neighbor on the ship. More than one thousand children were orphaned by the sinking. Calvary Cemetery in Milwaukee erected a monument to the tragedy and the many victims who are buried there, and in 1996, the City of Milwaukee dedicated a lakefront plaque to commemorate the disaster.

In 1989, salvage diver Harry Zych discovered the remains of the ship several miles north of Winnetka, off the coast of Highwood, Illinois. It is in about sixty feet of water and consists of four main wreckage fields. Zych wanted to remove and preserve artifacts for public viewing through his nonprofit Lady Elgin Foundation, but the State of Illinois wanted it kept intact as an archaeological site. After more than ten years of protracted court battles, Zych finally won the rights to the wreck. Unfortunately, during the legal scuffling, the exact coordinates of the site were leaked to the sport diving community, and unethical scavengers descended on the wreck and stole many priceless artifacts. Today, no diving is permitted in the area without permission from Harry Zych or the Lady Elgin Foundation.

In the 150 years that have passed since that fateful night, the elements and curious divers have all taken their toll, and precious little remains of the once proud ship. The memories of the tragedy and the stories of those who were grievously affected by it live on, however, and remind us of the dangers of underestimating the power of the Great Lake Michigan.

Part III
PLANES, TRAINS AND AUTOMOBILES

AMERICAN AIRLINES FLIGHT 191

*Look, look, he blew an engine off! Equipment, I need equipment, he blew
an engine! Oh, shit...he's not talkin' to me...There he goes, there he goes...
—recording of O'Hare air traffic controller to colleagues after his
unsuccessful attempt to communicate with the doomed plane*

May 25, 1979, was a beautiful spring day in Chicago—sunny and sixty-three
degrees, with a brisk twenty-two-knot breeze from the northeast gusting
across the tarmac at O'Hare International Airport. At the time, O'Hare was
the world's busiest airport for takeoffs and landings, a distinction it would
maintain until federal flight caps imposed in 2004 caused Hartsfield-Jackson
International in Atlanta to edge into the top spot. More than 40 million
passengers and more than 1 million tons of mail and freight moved through
O'Hare in 1979, and by 2005, those numbers had nearly doubled. It remains
the nation's only dual-hub airport, serving as a hub for both United and
American Airlines.

The airport sits on a tract of land covering more than seven thousand
acres, about seventeen miles northwest of Chicago's downtown, in what
was once a small unincorporated community known as Orchard Place.
In the 1940s, the site housed a 2-million-square-foot manufacturing plant
for Douglas C-54s used during World War II, and the small airport was
known as Orchard Place Airport/Douglas Field. To this day, O'Hare

American Airlines DC-10, tail number N110AA, before its deadly crash.

still carries the three-letter FAA airport designator of "ORD." In 1945, Douglas Aircraft Company consolidated its manufacturing on the West Coast, and the City of Chicago looked to the nearly abandoned airfield as a future jetport that could replace the cramped and small Chicago Midway International Airport.

The land was not part of Chicago and wasn't even contiguous to the city. But the city fathers, loath to give up the control (and the tax dollars) generated by a major airport, quickly annexed a two-hundred-foot-wide strip of land through suburban Rosemont and Schiller Park to municipally connect the new development to Chicago. In 1949, the field was renamed O'Hare International Airport after Lieutenant Commander Edward "Butch" O'Hare, a World War II navy flying ace who won the Medal of Honor for his bravery in battle. Butch's father, Edward J. O'Hare, had achieved notoriety in a different fashion—he spent many years as an attorney for gangster Al Capone before he had a change of heart and helped federal prosecutors convict Capone of tax evasion, an act that ultimately cost him his life in a hail of gangland gunfire.

Of course, none of that mattered to the passengers on board American Airlines Flight 191 that May afternoon. It was the beginning of the long

Memorial Day weekend, and travelers on the Chicago to Los Angeles route were settling in for the three-and-a-half-hour direct flight. The plane was filled nearly to capacity with 258 passengers and a crew of 13. Several of the passengers were on their way to the American Booksellers Association annual convention at the Los Angeles Convention Center. Among them were *Playboy* magazine's managing editor Sheldon Wax; his wife, author Judith Wax; and the magazine's fiction editor, Vicki Haider. Also on board was Itzhak Bentov, the inventor of the cardiac catheter, and Leonard Stogel, a music business producer for such once popular groups as the Cowsills and Sam the Sham and the Pharaohs.

It was a routine flight for the experienced crew. The pilot was Captain Walter Lux, fifty-three, with 25,000 flight hours, almost 3,000 of them in the DC-10 aircraft. Also on the flight deck were First Officer James Dillard, forty-nine, and Flight Engineer Alfred Udovich, fifty-six, who had 25,000 flying hours between them, about 1,500 in DC-10s. In the cabin, a crew of ten flight attendants prepared the passengers for takeoff. With a seasoned crew, perfect weather and a modern and seemingly well-maintained aircraft, the flight promised to be a pleasant one for those on board.

At about 2:50 p.m., the McDonnell-Douglas DC-10-10, tail number N110AA, backed away from gate K5 and was cleared to taxi to runway 32R. At 2:59 p.m., it was taxied into position and held for takeoff clearance. With full fuel tanks and a nearly full load of passengers, the DC-10's takeoff weight was about 379,000 pounds. It had plenty of room to maneuver on

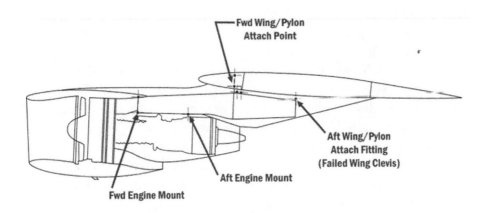

Drawing of the DC-10's engine mounting system, showing the failed aft wing attachment point.

32R, however, which was the airport's second-longest runway at slightly over ten thousand feet in length. At 3:02 p.m., the plane was cleared for takeoff and began to rumble down the asphalt. American Airlines had recently introduced a new passenger perk, the ability to watch the plane's takeoff and landing aboard the aircraft on closed-circuit television. If any of the passengers were watching, what they saw next surely horrified them.

About six thousand feet into the takeoff roll, just as the giant aircraft began to lift away from the ground, the no. 1 port engine and its mounting pylon suddenly tore loose from the left wing. Still generating massive thrust, the engine careened up and over the wing, somersaulting to the blacktop below. Air traffic controllers watching the takeoff immediately tried to contact the flight in hopes it could return for an emergency landing, but the calls were met with silence. The tower could do nothing but watch helplessly and begin the call for emergency equipment.

For a brief moment, the plane continued to climb normally, although it was spewing a vapor trail of fuel and hydraulic fluids. In the cockpit, the pilot and copilot would only be aware that they had lost power in the no. 1 engine. The wing-mounted engine was set far back, well out of visual range of the flight crew. They would have had no indication that the engine had completely torn away, taking with it a three-foot section of the wing's leading edge and ripping away vital hydraulic and electric lines that operated some of the airplane's control surfaces and powered parts of the cockpit instrument panel. The three-engine DC-10 was capable of flying with complete power loss to one of its engines, and pilots train frequently for such an occurrence. By all indications, the crew of Flight 191 followed engine-out emergency procedures exactly. Unfortunately, they had no way of knowing that they weren't dealing with a simple engine power failure.

As the hydraulic system lost power, the wing slats on the outboard edge of the damaged left wing began to retract under the air load. These slats allow a plane's wing to maintain lift at lower speeds; when they fail (or are intentionally retracted), the wing requires more speed to keep it aloft. In keeping with emergency engine failure procedures, the crew raised the nose of the jet up to fourteen degrees, which reduced the airspeed from 165 knots to 153 knots. But now, unknown to the pilot, the damaged left wing required about 159 knots or more to maintain lift. The slat disagreement system and the "stick-shaker" stall warning had both been disabled by the wing damage, leaving the crew virtually blind to the circumstances surrounding the craft.

When the plane reached an altitude of about four hundred feet above ground, the left wing aerodynamically stalled and lost lift. The right wing was still flying, creating a situation known as asymmetric lift. In layman's terms, it meant that the left wing of the plane dropped suddenly toward the ground, while the right wing briefly continued to pull the plane forward through the air, causing the aircraft to flip onto its side. About thirty-one seconds into its flight—which seemed like a lifetime to those watching in horror from the ground—Flight 191 clipped the ground with its left wingtip and slammed nose-first into an abandoned airfield and old aircraft hangar less than a mile from the end of the runway.

The explosion could be heard and felt from many miles away. Some residents of nearby towns thought at first that it was an earthquake, but the oily black cloud that mushroomed hundreds of feet into the sky quickly signified the true disaster. Emergency crews were on the scene almost immediately; indeed, some had started rolling while the plane was still airborne. The first responders were trained to look for survivors, but what they found instead was a field filled with small, charred bits of debris and body parts. A Roman Catholic priest who arrived moments after the crash told the *Chicago Tribune*: "It was too hot to really do anything but administer the last rites. I just walked around trying to touch a body here or there, but I could not. It was too hot to touch anybody, and I really could not tell if they were men or women."

As rescuers searched through the scene, they discovered that Flight 191 had also claimed victims on the ground. Two employees at the nearby Courtney Velo Excavating Company's repair garage were killed by flaming debris, and

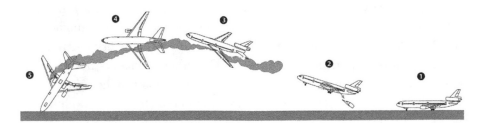

The final flight path of American Airlines Flight 191. 1) 191 begins takeoff roll; 2) left engine rips loose and flips over wing; 3) plane appears to climb normally, but smoke and hydraulic fluid stream from damaged wing; 4) left wing loses lift, stalls and drops, flipping the plane onto its side at a 112-degree angle; 5) after wingtip clips the ground, plane slams nose-first into an empty field. *Illustration by Brian Diskin.*

two more were severely burned. The company had been operating out of the old hangar, which had once been part of the long-deserted Ravenswood Airport. The wreckage came to rest just yards away from the adjacent and crowded Oasis Mobile Home Trailer Park, where a few homes and numerous cars were destroyed. Had it hit the park directly, the loss of life would have been even more catastrophic. Of the 273 victims, rescuers were only able to recover 12 intact bodies.

The National Transportation Safety Board (NTSB) and Federal Bureau of Investigation (FBI) quickly arrived on the scene to investigate. Air traffic controller Ed Rucker claimed that he saw a "flash" from the wing, which led to some concerns about a terrorist bomb. More than sixty witnesses on the airfield, however, had a clearer view of the engine separating and flipping over the wing. Another bit of confusion occurred when investigators began to comb the crash site and discovered charred pieces of a small private plane. Although none had been reported in the area, investigators wondered if one had unwittingly intruded into the flight path as the big jet was struggling to stay aloft. Early news pictures show NTSB vice-chairman Elwood T. Driver standing in the debris field, ominously displaying a broken nut and bolt to the press as if he held the answer to the disaster in his hand. That concern was quickly explained away when they discovered that a small aircraft parts broker was still operating out of one of the old Ravenswood hangars and that the pieces they found were simply parts that had scattered and burned when Flight 191 hit the hangar.

Ultimately, investigators traced the disaster back to several different problems that combined to create the "perfect storm" and cause the crash. To begin, NTSB blamed maintenance procedures that were performed on the plane about eight weeks earlier at American Airlines' maintenance facility in Tulsa, Oklahoma, when engine no. 1 was removed for servicing. The manufacturer, McDonnell-Douglas, recommended that engines be removed first and then the mounting pylon, separately from the wing. The airline mechanics, however, had developed a procedure to remove the engine and pylon together as one unit. It seemed like a safe innovation; it reduced man-hours by nearly two hundred hours and reduced the number of required disconnects of vital fuel, electric and hydraulic lines from seventy-two to twenty-seven. Many airlines used the new maintenance procedure, including American, Continental and United.

The procedure involved using a forklift (or, in the case of United, a hoist) to steady the engine and pylon assembly as mechanics removed it. It was a delicate process, however, and any misstep could cause the assembly to seesaw against the wing and cause stress fractures in the mounting. In the case of AA no. N110AA, the engine removal was in progress during a shift change. When the new shift began work, they found that the forklift had shifted and needed to be repositioned. This movement caused a small, unnoticed crack in the housing attachment. Over the course of several weeks, the crack worsened, until the assembly finally failed completely during Flight 191's takeoff.

The loss of an engine in this manner would not, by itself, have doomed the flight. The well-trained pilots could have flown the plane with two engines and returned safely for an emergency landing. Unfortunately, the severe damage to the hydraulic and electric lines in the left wing caused other critical handicaps by effectively blinding the pilot with a loss of vital instrumentation and drastically raising the stall speed of the damaged wing. Ironically, it was the pilot's careful adherence to emergency procedures that ultimately caused the fatal stall. In the wake of the disaster, the procedures were quickly amended to allow pilots in similar engine-out situations to maintain, rather than reduce, their speed.

After investigators discovered the damaged pylon assembly, the Federal Aviation Administration (FAA) immediately grounded all DC-10s for inspection. Six of the grounded planes were found to have similar cracks—four American Airlines aircraft and two Continental aircraft. Interestingly, none of the United planes—which used a similar maintenance procedure but used a hoist instead of a forklift—had any damage. In the end, the NTSB spread the blame rather widely. The airline and its maintenance facility, the manufacturer, the FAA and the airline industry itself all shouldered part of the responsibility, according to the final report. American Airlines was fined $500,000 for improper maintenance procedures, and Continental Airlines was fined $100,000 on a similar charge. Few, if any, DC-10s remain in passenger service in the United States today, but they are popular cargo planes, used by operators such as FedEx and UPS.

Although more than thirty years have passed since the disaster, Flight 191 retains the dubious distinction of being the worst single plane crash in history on U.S. soil. (The *intentional* terrorist crashes of 9/11 are not in this category.) There is no monument to those who died, although family and friends still fight to have one erected. Even without a monument, however, those who lived in Chicago in 1979 no doubt will never forget the horrendous images from that tragic day.

THE 1972 ILLINOIS CENTRAL TRAIN CRASH

I don't think any relatives would want to see what is downstairs [in the morgue].

—Dr. Andrew J. Toman, coroner

Monday, October 30, 1972, was a gray and cloudy morning as commuters began a new week's trek into schools and offices across the city. Some sat impatiently in endless exhaust-filled traffic jams in their automobiles; others lumbered along on the bulky city buses, bouncing over the inevitable potholes that never seemed to disappear no matter how much asphalt the city workers shoveled into their insatiable maws. Yet others started the morning in the relative comfort of one of the modern commuter trains that rolled into Chicago each morning from points as far away as Kenosha, Wisconsin. The next day was Halloween, and many people would be thinking about parties and costumes and candy for the kids.

At about 7:06 a.m., Illinois Central train no. 416 left the South Chicago Station at 93rd Street for its morning run into the city. The train was made up of four of the brand-new lightweight double-decker Highliner cars, each with a capacity of 156 passengers. Built in 1971 by the St. Louis Car Company, the new cars were lighter, faster and able to carry more passengers than the old single heavyweight cars they were slowly replacing. The new cars operated on the same electric catenary (overhead wires) used by the old cars, and they were painted orange, dark brown and silver in keeping with Illinois Central's corporate colors.

Number 416 was running slightly behind schedule as it neared the 27th Street Station. That station is known as a "flag stop," which meant the train did not stop unless a passenger wished to board or disembark there. That morning, a passenger notified the crew that he wanted to get off at 27th Street. The conductor in charge of the train was Ernest R. Cummings, and engineer James A. Watts and collector Jeremiah J. O'Connell rounded out the crew. The train overshot the station by several hundred feet and proceeded to back up. The crew seemed to ignore the fact that once they had begun to back into the station, their train had triggered a green light signal at 27th Street, signifying that the track was clear, while the signal at 31st Street to the south changed from yellow to red. In such cases, safety rules clearly state that the crew of a

The Illinois Central train crash. Many victims were saved because of the fast response from doctors and nurses at Michael Reese Hospital, the dark-colored building at rear of photo.

stopped or backing train must communicate in some manner—either by radio or by flagman—to prevent approaching trains from entering or moving within the same signal block area.

On that morning, the crew of no. 416 reportedly made no attempt to send a flagman down the tracks. Perhaps they thought that no other trains were close behind, or perhaps they were hesitant to walk the muddy and cold tracks in the overcast morning fog and drizzle. Maybe they thought that the red signal at 31st Street would stop any approaching trains. Some union officials later claimed that the safety rule was never enforced and that trains weren't even equipped with flagging equipment such as flares and flags. In any case, their lapse was a deadly one.

Bearing down on the 27th Street Station was train no. 720, an express train made up of six older, single-level cars constructed of heavy steel. The steel cars were seventy-two feet long, with a passenger capacity of 84. That day, both trains were filled to capacity and had standing passengers, with a combined estimated total of about 1,100 commuters. Number 720 had no functioning speedometer, but Robert W. Cavanaugh, the engineer, testified that he was slowing his train to about thirty miles per hour in compliance with the yellow caution light he saw at 31st Street. Later investigators agreed with his speed estimate. As Cavanaugh passed the 31st Street signal, he would not have seen it turning red to warn of the backing up train ahead. At that point, his view would have been of the next signal north of 27th Street, which had turned green as no. 416 backed away from it. Since his train was an express, the engineer did not need to stop at the station and could proceed past at a safe speed. The tracks leading into the area curved to the west, limiting the engineer's forward view, but the green light ahead told him that it was safe to continue.

As no. 720 rounded the curve, Cavanaugh was horrified to see the dark shape of another train looming on the tracks directly in front of him. Visibility was poor that day, with fog and drizzle, and the new Highliner's paint scheme of dark brown on the rear of the cars made it especially hard to see until the last moment. The engineer applied the brake so hard that he snapped off the brake lever. He also reversed the train's electric motors, but it was too late. The old steel cars slammed into the new train, telescoping deep into the rear of the lightweight Highliner. Seconds before the collision, conductor Cummings of no. 416 jumped from the cab of his train onto the platform, leaving his passengers to suffer their fate alone. Cavanaugh was not as lucky and was hospitalized in serious condition with multiple fractures and other injuries.

The damage was devastating. One passenger in the front of the double-decker train said that the rear car "collapsed like tinfoil" in the collision, trapping and killing dozens upon impact. Fortunately, the accident occurred less than a hundred yards from Michael Reese Hospital and only a short distance away from nearby Mercy Hospital. Doctors and nurses from both facilities heard the crash, ran to the scene and were rescuing and triaging victims even before the police and fire crews arrived. Medical personnel set up a primitive emergency ward on the station's platform, where they did their best to sort and stabilize the victims for transport. More than 240 firemen and dozens of police squadrols and ambulances responded to the scene, along with two helicopters.

It was a grisly scene. The *Chicago Tribune* called it "one of the bloodiest accidents in the city's history," and it remains today the deadliest train wreck ever to occur in Chicago. Many of the victims were decapitated, and some bodies were sliced in half. Rescuers bundled the remains into bloodied blankets and placed them in police squadrols, saving the ambulances for those still clinging to life. Workers at the Cook County (Chicago) Morgue on West

Polk Street watched in sadness and disbelief as a seemingly endless stream of blue and white police vehicles—emergency lights flashing but sirens silent—backed up to the morgue's delivery dock with their heart-rending bundles.

The remains were brought to the identification room on the lower floor, where workers fingerprinted the corpses if possible and searched for any other clues that would assist them in putting a name or description on the body. A Roman Catholic priest, Father John Mahoney, walked amongst the gurneys and offered prayers and the sacrament of Anointing the Sick (Last Rites) to each of the victims. Father Mahoney later said, "I don't know who was Catholic and who was not, but God will sort it out."

By that afternoon, all of the bodies had been removed from the wreckage, but the devastating physical and emotional toll on the victims and their families was just beginning. There were so many injured that they were taken to seven Chicago area hospitals, in order to prevent any facility from becoming overwhelmed. Televisions and newspapers broadcast a call for blood donors to assist with the grave need. For relatives and friends, it was a nightmarish search to find their loved ones. Many of the injured were unconscious or too badly hurt to offer their names, so some were simply given numbers until they could be identified later. Families traveled from hospital to hospital or sat in terror by the telephone, hoping and praying for good news.

Others made a grief-stricken pilgrimage to the morgue, where they sat on hard wooden benches as the grim work in the basement dragged on. Due to the carnage, people were not allowed to view the bodies in an attempt to confirm identity, except in the rare cases where the deceased was relatively unscarred. Some victims were tentatively identified by clothing or jewelry, giving the family at least temporary solace that their husband or son or daughter or mother had been found. Many weren't so fortunate and had to suffer for days until dental records confirmed the sad news.

In the final tally, forty-five people died and nearly four hundred were injured. Many of the dead were students heading to the various city colleges. Others were downtown office workers preparing for another week on the job. Each had their own unique story. Two sisters traveling together were separated when one girl sat in a different car to talk with a friend she had spotted. One sister died; the other escaped completely unharmed. Another young victim had purchased a double indemnity life insurance policy just weeks before, teasing his mother that she would be rich if he died. One girl was on her way downtown for her first day at a new job. A young father of infant twin girls was among the dead.

An Illinois Central Highliner train. These lightweight double-decker cars were modern and efficient but, according to a witness, "crumpled like tinfoil" in the crash.

After investigation, the NTSB ruled as follows: "The National Transportation Safety Board determines that the probable cause of the accident was the reverse movement of train 416 (the lead train) without flag protection into a previously vacated signal block and the failure of the engineer of train 720 (the following train), to perceive the train ahead in time to avoid the collision." As a direct result of the disaster, all Chicago train lines now paint the rear of their cars a high-visibility orange, and many include reflective striping. Due to the curve in the tracks and the green signal ahead, however, it's doubtful that this measure would have done much to change the outcome of the catastrophic 1972 crash.

THE 1977 LOOP EL CRASH

I saw a couple of people who were underneath the [falling] *car trying to run, but they didn't make it*

—*Renel Conner, witness*

Chicago is a city that is largely defined by its transportation systems. A railroad hub, a dual airline hub, a ship's port, a crossroads for numerous interstate highways—Chicago is movement, a city perpetually on the go.

Even its famed downtown area, the Loop, is named for the elevated rapid transit lines that circle its heart. Of course, like many cities, Chicago speaks in its own shorthand. No one ever mentions Lake Michigan; "the lake" will suffice. "The airport" typically means O'Hare, even though Midway, Chicago's secondary airport, does a healthy business on its own.

And those rapid transit lines? The el. Even the subways are usually called the el, because they eventually climb above ground at one point or another. The deafening rumble as one of these trains passes overhead is just part of life in the city. Even the multitudes of pigeons perched underneath the tracks barely glance up as the monsters roar past. After all, it's just the el.

During the peak of rush hour on Friday, February 4, 1977, throngs of commuters were flooding into various el lines for the trip home. It was the end of a cold and dreary workweek, and most of the riders probably looked forward to the warmth and comfort of home. The temperature was only in the twenties, and a snowstorm that had already dumped four inches on the city was still sputtering intermittently. High overhead, the clatter and rumble of passing trains made conversation on the street difficult.

CTA elevated trains (known as the El) on the northeast corner of the Loop. Here the tracks make a ninety-degree turn from Wabash to Lake. *Wikimedia photo.*

That afternoon, the Chicago Transit Authority (CTA) had experienced some switching problems, due in part to ice on the tracks. With multiple tracks, the CTA could run extra trains either outbound or inbound, depending on the demand. It also eliminated some station delays, because the various lines could run in opposing directions around the Loop, thus using different platforms to pick up and discharge their passengers. On that day, however, the switch problem forced the Evanston Express, which normally ran in a clockwise circle, to share tracks with the Ravenswood and westbound Lake–Dan Ryan trains, running in a counterclockwise route. It wasn't a safety issue, but it did promise to make that evening's commute slower than normal.

Shortly after 5:20 p.m., a six-car Ravenswood line train bound for the northwest side of the city pulled away from the Randolph Street Station on Wabash Avenue and made the ninety-degree turn from Wabash onto Lake Street, approaching the State Street stop. An Evanston Express was picking up passengers at State Street, so the Ravenswood motorman stopped his train just short of the platform and waited for the other train to clear the station. At about the same time, an eight-car Lake–Dan Ryan train headed for the West Side approached from behind. There was no reason for concern. In addition to the track signals, each train was also equipped with cab signals to let the motorman know of other trains in the vicinity. Besides, the speed limit on the curve was just fifteen miles per hour, so trains in the area typically moved at a crawl.

As passengers and witnesses watched in surprise, the approaching train continued to creep forward around the bend in the tracks, ignoring all the signals, until it bumped into the stopped Ravenswood train. Due to the slow speed of the impact, the passengers felt just a barely perceptible thump. What happened next, however, was as mystifying as it was horrific.

The motorman of the Lake–Dan Ryan train, Stephan A. Martin, having just struck the train ahead of him, inexplicably began to apply full forward traction, seemingly in an attempt to push the stopped Ravenswood cars ahead down the tracks. The eight cars of his train were curved around the bend, with the cab facing west on Lake Street, while the rear cars were still pointed north on Wabash. As the wheels of the cars fiercely gripped the tracks in response to his command, the train began to rock and seesaw in its attempt to move forward. The Ravenswood train was pushed off the rails by its assailant, but it remained upright on the track. The Lake–Dan Ryan train was not as lucky. Above the roar of screeching metal and shooting sparks, the passengers screamed in panic as the swaying and bucking cars, unable to move forward as commanded, began to jackknife on the tracks. The coupling bars between the first three cars bent and twisted, driving the car ends upward. The rear cars, still desperately trying to forge ahead, shoved the front cars completely off the tracks, and they tumbled over twenty feet to the distant pavement.

Terrified pedestrians on the busy street below scrambled for safety as the massive train fell toward them, but some weren't able to escape in time. The first and third cars landed flat on their sides in the middle of Wabash Avenue. The second car fell against the track supports and stood on end, tumbling passengers and seats into a wounded and panicked heap. The fourth car landed partially atop car number three, its rear end dangling precipitously from the tracks, hanging only by the coupling bar that still tethered it to car number five. The rear cars derailed but remained on the tracks.

The scene on the street was one of shattered glass, twisted metal and blood. Some of the passengers were ejected from the falling cars and lay dead or injured on the pavement. An unlucky few fell out, only to have a toppling car land on top of them. Passersby and customers from a nearby restaurant rushed to help, leading dazed and bloodied people out of the cold and snow and into the restaurant, which was quickly pressed into service as a temporary emergency room.

When police and fire emergency units arrived moments later, they were faced with a scene of complete chaos. Hundreds of terrified and injured passengers were still trapped in the wreckage, some still hanging helplessly in the air. On the street, they began to pull the least injured to safety through the shattered windows of the prone cars. Others were imprisoned by pieces of twisted metal and had to be freed by rescuers with chain saws and blowtorches. A fire department snorkel and ladder unit worked to pluck victims from the dangling fourth car.

Television reporters and other news crews descended on the scene, capturing images of the carnage. One picture, taken an hour after the crash, showed the legs of a victims sticking out from beneath one of the fallen cars. Ultimately, it would take emergency personnel several hours to free the living and retrieve the dead. The blowing snow and bitterly cold wind made the rescue all the more difficult and added to the discomfort of the injured. The Chicago Police Department put out a desperate request for doctors and

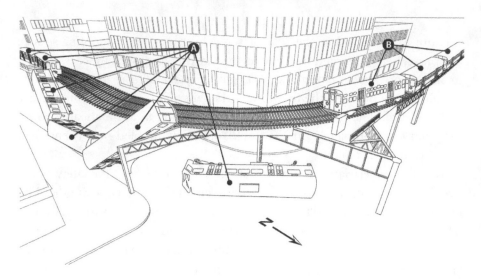

Diagram of the Loop El crash. B) Ravenswood train heading west on Lake Street was stopped on the tracks, waiting for another train to clear the State Street Station. A) Lake–Dan Ryan train turning onto Lake from Wabash gently rear-ended the Ravenswood train but then inexplicably attempted to accelerate forward. The force derailed the Ravenswood train, but it remained on the tracks. The accelerating Lake–Dan Ryan train derailed, and its first four cars fell to the street below. *Illustration by Brian Diskin.*

blood donors as the casualties mounted. The final toll was eleven dead and nearly two hundred injured, many quite seriously.

Over and over, those involved in the crash—either as witnesses or passengers—repeated the same words: "It happened so fast!" One moment they were routinely making their way home on a typical Friday evening, when suddenly and without warning disaster struck. And a senseless disaster at that. CTA officials suspected a mechanical problem, such as a signal malfunction; what else could explain such an accident? The National Transportation Safety Board in Washington said it would take on the investigation, but the CTA appointed its own investigative panel as well.

What they discovered was surprising: there had been no system malfunction and no equipment failure. The motorman, Stephan Martin, was simply high on drugs at the time of the crash. He admitted to smoking marijuana before he came on duty and had four marijuana joints in his backpack when police interviewed him after the tragedy. It wasn't his first violation; he had been disciplined in the past for safety issues, including a previous derailment that was his fault. Apparently, as Martin rounded the curve onto Lake Street that evening, he had ignored or overridden the safety controls in his cab and proceeded against the signals. When he bumped the Ravenswood train, he reacted in either panic or confusion and pushed controls forward, causing his train to lurch ahead.

In response to the disaster, the CTA issued a directive forbidding motormen to proceed past a red signal without permission from the Control Center. Motormen had previously been allowed to use their judgment and advance cautiously through a signal, shortening the distance between themselves and another train in an effort to save time. Although the new rule was an obvious reaction to the accident, it's unlikely that it would have changed the fates of that February day. The motorman was seriously impaired, and no regulatory dictum would have made him any more clearheaded. Unfortunately for the hundreds of passengers who put their trust in him, his poor choices became their nightmare on that snowy Chicago day.

Part IV
THE WRATH OF GOD

THE 1954 CHICAGO SEICHE

*It didn't come in like a wall...the water just started to rise and kept going
until it was maybe 6 feet higher than usual.*
—Dick Keating, Belmont Harbor foreman, in a newspaper account

Although native Chicagoans frequently joke that we have only two seasons—winter and construction—Chicago actually enjoys its share of beautiful weather, especially in late spring and early summer. On these glorious days, the robin's-egg blue sky meets the sparkling deep blue waters of Lake Michigan in a view to infinity, while gentle breezes off the lake mitigate the heat of the brilliant sunlight dancing on the waves. It's a great time to bike or stroll the lakefront—or, in the long tradition of our hunter-gatherer ancestors, go fishing.

June 26, 1954, was just such a day. That Saturday morning dawned sunny and clear, and the fishermen plied the waterfront in droves, hoping for that perfect trout or perch dinner to appear. Earlier, forecasters had warned of severe weather on the Michigan and Indiana portions of the lake, but Chicago seemed to be spared. A line of severe squalls and high winds had swept from LaCrosse, Wisconsin, in the northwest to the southeast that morning, pounding the shoreline of Michigan City, Indiana, with waves up to six feet tall. In Chicago, however, there was no trace of rain—just a peaceful and warm day perfect for enjoying the water.

The word "seiche" (pronounced *saysh*) is derived from a regional Swiss French word meaning "to sway back and forth." The term was first used by Swiss scientist François-Alphonse Forel, who used it to describe water oscillation in alpine lakes. Forel was known as the father of limnology (the study of inland waters), and he spent a great deal of time observing and calculating seiche activity on Lake Geneva. Seiches form when a disturbance, typically from wind or atmospheric pressure, pushes aside water in an enclosed or partially enclosed basin, such as a lake or bay. As gravity tries to pull the water back to level, it causes a rhythmic back-and-forth motion. Visualize bumping into a pan of water: the initial wave caused by your action sloshes back and forth across the surface until it gradually subsides. That is, in essence, a miniature seiche.

Seiches are often confused with tsunamis, but the two are quite different. Tsunamis are usually caused by seismic activity such as underwater earthquakes or volcanic eruptions. The sudden disturbance in the water causes a series of high-energy waves that can move across the ocean at

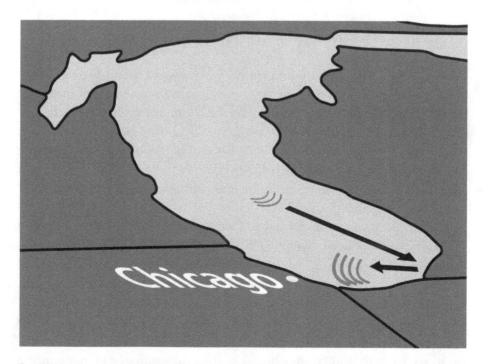

In 1954, a severe storm in Lake Michigan traveled from the northwest to the southeast, pushing heavy waves against the shorelines of Indiana and Michigan and creating a seiche that killed people along the shore in Chicago. *Illustration by Brian Diskin.*

speeds of up to five hundred miles per hour. In deep water, tsunamis are nearly invisible and will pass under boats without being noticed. When those waves begin to pile up in shallow water, however, a massive wall of water can result. Seiches, on the other hand, tend to move comparatively slowly through the water. When a seiche reaches shore, it creates a sudden rise in the water level, rather than the killer wave often depicted in some accounts. Even though its appearance is often less dramatic, that doesn't mean a seiche is any less deadly.

On that lovely summer morning, there was no warning of the disaster that was about to occur. About fifty people were fishing on the Montrose Harbor breakwater, which stretches in a fishhook shape off the beach. About 9:25 a.m., as anglers lazily tended their lines, the choppy waves suddenly began to climb toward their feet. The top of the breakwater is usually about four or five feet above the surface of the lake, but now the water swelled upward to engulf everything in its path. Dozens were swept into the water, while others held fast to whatever surface they could grab. Witnesses agreed that the water reached a height of about five feet above the breakwater at its peak, meaning that the surge was possibly ten feet in height, and it was estimated at twenty-five miles wide, stretching from Jackson Park on the south up to suburban Wilmette on the north.

The water receded as quickly as it had risen, leaving people who had just minutes ago been standing on solid ground now floundering in the lake. Some were able to swim to shore on their own, and others were plucked from the water by people on the beach who quickly raced to the rescue. Nearby pleasure boats rode out the swell safely and aided in rescuing those in the water. At the same time, four Coast Guard ships had been cruising the lakefront awaiting the arrival of the submarine *U-505*. Once radioed about the disaster, they immediately diverted to Montrose Harbor to aid in search and rescue.

At the North Avenue beach, the scene was similar. There were only a dozen or so fishermen on the pier, but about a hundred beachgoers began to scream and run for safety as the water started to rise. The swell crawled about 150 feet onshore, flooding the crowded beach with about 2 feet of water and debris and floating the rowboats used for rescue. Joseph Pecararo, a twenty-four-year-old lifeguard captain, was struggling to pull the scattered lifeboats onto higher ground when someone shouted that one of the fishermen had been swept away. John Jaworski, fishing with his eighteen-year-old son Joseph,

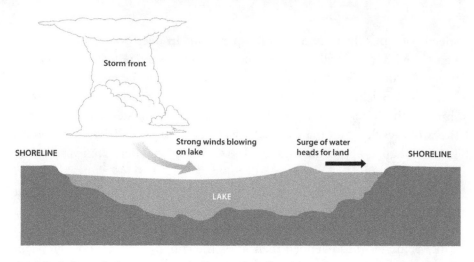

A seiche is formed when a strong wind or another disturbance forces water to one side of an enclosed area, such as a lake or bay. As the water seeks to level itself, it "sloshes" back to the opposite shore and creates a sudden but temporary rise in the water level. Seiches in lakes happen frequently but are rarely significant enough to cause trouble. *Illustration by Brian Diskin.*

had disappeared. Two other lifeguards, Joseph Delmonico and Lawrence Hoffman, spotted the fifty-two-year-old year old Jaworski struggling in the water and dove into the surf to rescue him. He was unconscious when the lifeguards pulled him to shore and failed to respond to resuscitation efforts. Jaworski was the only fatality at North Avenue.

Back at Montrose, some of the survivors were injured or in shock from the ordeal, and many people were missing and unaccounted for. At first, rescuers feared that up to thirty people might have been swept to their deaths. Doctors from the American Hospital rushed to the scene to administer first aid. The lifeguards from North Avenue beach, satisfied that everyone at that location was safe and accounted for, raced to Montrose to help. One of the first victims recovered at Montrose was Mrs. Mae Gabriel, forty-eight, a mother of eleven children. According to some accounts, Mrs. Gabriel had been pulled from the water earlier but had returned in an attempt to rescue her husband Edward, forty-nine. Sadly, she was unsuccessful. Her body was recovered quickly, but Edward wasn't found until some days later.

Another fatality was Theodore Stempinski, who had gone fishing that beautiful morning with his sixteen-year-old son, Ralph. Mr. Stempinski had not purchased a fishing license that day and had received a ticket from Herbert Riederer, then a twenty-four-year-old state conservation officer. While

Riederer wrote the ticket, Ralph walked off the pier and went to the nearby boathouse. As the conservation officer walked toward the shoreline, he heard a rush of water and looked back just in time to see people swept from the pier. He did not have a radio to report the disaster, so he ran to the roadway and commandeered a car to drive him to the nearest telephone, located at the bait shop half a mile away. Ralph heard the commotion and ran back outside, but it was too late —his father was gone. A bystander, Tony Kudelko, swam out 150 feet in an attempt to save Stempinski, but the man had already drowned. Kudelko and three other rescuers brought the lifeless body to shore.

James Kay was luckier. The fifty-year-old fisherman had been swept off the breakwater and carried to the mouth of the harbor. As he struggled in exhaustion to remain afloat, a twenty-one-foot cabin cruiser named *Sarida* was hurrying to shore after spotting the massive swell. As the crew slowed to maneuver through the debris now floating in the water, they spotted Kay, tossed him life preservers and hauled him on board. Kay had been fishing with his son-in-law, Earl Gerhardt. Gerhardt managed to cling to a piling until the water receded, and both men were quickly reunited with their wives, who had watched in horror from the beach as the men disappeared into the water.

News of the disaster quickly spread throughout the Chicago park system, and lifeguards at other beaches along the shoreline had time to warn people away from the water. In Jackson Park, police cleared fishermen from a pier at 61st Street just moments before the water struck and submerged that pier. At Oak Street beach, the swell pushed lifeboats seventy-five feet inland, all the way up to Lake Shore Drive, but no one was injured.

By the time police and the Coast Guard arrived on the scene at Montrose, their role was one of recovery, not rescue. Of course, the recovery effort was not easy, either. Strong cross currents made diving especially dangerous, and the disturbed sediment reduced visibility to about six inches. Divers literally had to crawl through the water blindly, operating by feel. It was several days before all victims were accounted for.

In total, eight people died in the unusual tragedy that sunny June morning: one at North Avenue and seven at Montrose Avenue. The fatalities, however, could easily have been much higher if not for the heroic acts of ordinary citizens. Most of the early rescuers were fishermen or beachgoers who risked their own lives in order to save the lives of strangers. The city, for its part, responded to the disaster by installing "seiche fences" along many of the

North Avenue beach and pier in Chicago. The cable and steel post "seiche fence" on the pier is a result of the 1954 deaths. It is designed to offer an emergency handhold in the event of sudden waves or surges. *Wikimedia photo.*

lakefront piers and breakwaters. These are metal posts and cables anchored in concrete, designed to offer a safe handhold in the event of high waves or sudden water fluctuations.

Thankfully, Chicago hasn't experienced any major seiches since the 1954 killer, although minor episodes occur a few times a year. These go mostly unnoticed by Chicagoans, except perhaps by those old enough to remember and respect the deadly power of lakefront seiches. Meanwhile, in the event of another catastrophe, the seiche fences stand along the breakwaters like silent sentries, a grim reminder of a beautiful summer day long ago that went terribly wrong.

THE 1967 TORNADOES

I said a few prayers. I [said] *an Act of Contrition on that floor. When I got up, the bus in front of me was tipped over. The house beside me was off its foundation. I knew a lot of people were hurt. The whole area was flattened.*
—Belvidere police captain Francis Whalen

It seems that no matter where you live in the United States, you will be subjected to some quirk of weather or geology. The East Coast battles

hurricanes, the West Coast struggles against wildfires and earthquakes and the Midwest has its tornadoes. Most Chicago schoolchildren know the drill all too well: stay away from windows, go down into the basement or a small interior room on the lowest floor and get under a sturdy piece of furniture. Chicagoans also know the difference between a tornado watch (conditions are ripe for one to form) and a tornado warning (one has been spotted).

In reality, tornado watches—and even warnings—are so common in the Midwest, especially during the spring, that many residents barely pay them any notice. This dangerous complacency sometimes adds to injuries and fatalities when a monster storm actually does hit. Other times, even advance warnings and careful planning do little to mitigate the damage from these capricious acts of nature. And sometimes, the ferocious marauders drop from the sky with almost no warning, catching victims unprepared and helpless. On April 21, 1967, it was a combination of these scenarios that killed 58 people and left more than 1,500 injured in the deadliest tornado event to ever hit northern Illinois. (In August 1990, a tornado in Plainfield, Illinois, was more powerful and caused more property damage, but thankfully was responsible for fewer fatalities.)

On that warm and humid Friday afternoon, the National Weather Service issued a tornado watch at 1:50 p.m. for parts of the region, one of the first of many watches and warnings that would continue throughout the afternoon. A strong low-pressure system was moving north-northeast against a stationary front that stretched from northern Missouri to lower Michigan. The air mass was becoming extremely unstable, and several small funnel clouds were spotted against the dark greenish sky.

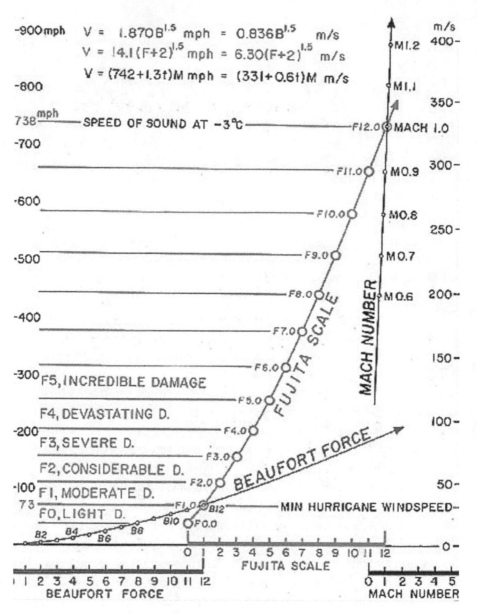

The Fujita scale for classifying tornadoes. On April 21, 1967, ten tornadoes raked across the Chicago area, including three deadly F4 storms.

In Belvidere, Illinois, schools were about to let out for the weekend. Belvidere is a town of about twenty-five thousand residents, located seventy-five miles northwest of downtown of Chicago and about twelve miles east of Rockford. The town is divided by the Kishwaukee River and was known for its massive Chrysler Automotive assembly plant. In 1967, the plant manufactured the Chrysler Newport and Plymouth Fury. Today, after a major restructuring and modernization, it produces the Dodge Caliber, Jeep Compass and Jeep Patriot.

Shortly before 3:50 p.m., a line of sixteen school buses idled in front of the nearly new Belvidere High School. The buses had first picked up grade school children at other schools and had just arrived to pick up the high schoolers. Some were nearly full, others just loading as lines of children queued up to get a seat. Suddenly, a dark shape loomed from the west, ripping up houses along nearby Highland Street. Children began to scream and run as the whirling blackness dropped down onto them. It was a deadly F4 tornado—some witnesses insist that there were two—and it was bearing down on the school. There was almost no time to react. Teachers tried to pull students back into the school as the buses flipped about like dried leaves in a breeze. One bus landed nearly a mile away from the school. Cars filled with parents waiting at the curb to pick up their kids were picked up by the storm and tumbled down the street. Some students and a police officer arriving at the scene survived by immediately dropping flat against the ground and waiting for the maelstrom to pass.

The school building itself was severely damaged. Almost all of the windows were blown out, and large chunks of the roof were missing. As teachers, parents and older students struggled in the driving rain to assist the injured and dying and search for the missing, the tornado continued on its relentless march to the northeast, cutting a path of destruction half a mile wide and about twenty-eight miles long to the northern Illinois town of Woodstock. It badly damaged the nearby Chrysler plant, where three hundred new cars and one hundred employee cars were destroyed. The twister completely demolished 127 homes and damaged several hundred more.

Back at the school, volunteers turned their cars into makeshift ambulances, racing injured children to nearby hospitals. One volunteer, Jim Bonner, told the *Rockford Register Star*: "I don't know how many I took to Highland Hospital. I would...back up the station wagon [at the school], and they'd shove them into the car. Then I'd just drive to the hospital where they took

An example of devastation from an F4 tornado.

them out. You couldn't tell how bad they were hurt. They were all rolled in mud." School officials quickly set up a triage system: the injured were placed in the cafeteria, severely injured in the library and the gym was reserved as a morgue for the dead. Parents filed through in horror, trying to find their lost children.

Highland Hospital, which took in about seventy-five of the injured, had also sustained damage in the storm, including the loss of all but four of its windows. It operated on emergency power and treated victims in the basement. Shortly after 7:00 p.m., it was forced to evacuate when the roof over the surgical wing began to sag and creak. Patients were transported to hospitals in Rockford, which were already strained to capacity due to storm injuries.

In the end, thirteen of the twenty-four fatalities and three hundred of the five hundred injuries from the tornado in Belvidere occurred at the high school. The storm system, however, was far from finished with its malevolent disruption.

At 5:03 p.m., another twister touched down near Fox River Grove and carved a nine-mile trail northeast through North Barrington and Lake

Zurich. Lake Zurich was hardest hit, with nearly one hundred homes, a school and several businesses destroyed, and hundreds more damaged. Witnesses later described much the same scene as in Belvidere: no visible funnel cloud and no roar; just low, black, swirling clouds that suddenly descended without warning and destroyed everything in their path. In 1967, the area wasn't heavily developed and was dotted with rolling hills and thick patches of trees. Many of those trees were destroyed or uprooted, leaving a visible swath of destruction across the landscape. Although there was tremendous property damage and many people injured in this second round of tornadoes, there was only one reported fatality in Lake Zurich.

Now the storm had a deadly finale planned for its day of destruction. At 5:00 p.m., as Chicago area residents arrived home and tuned in to watch news reports about the tragedy in Belvidere, the NWS issued a tornado warning for Cook County (Chicago and surrounding suburbs). At 5:24 p.m., a witness spotted a funnel dropping from a cloud just south of 99th Street and Willow Springs Road and quickly notified authorities. It passed eastward over LaGrange Road and finally touched down on the western edge of Palos Hills, where Moraine Valley Community College now stands. After damaging some homes and ripping up trees and power lines, it skipped over the Tri-State Tollway (I-294) and continued on a path to the east-northeast.

Along the way, it destroyed numerous homes and businesses, including a drive-in movie theater near Chicago Ridge. In less than an hour, the theater would have opened and would have been filled with cars. Instead, its screen lay destroyed, its steel supports twisted like cardboard. The steel speaker stands were plucked from the ground and scattered across the debris-filled lot. The tornado, now about a block wide and gaining strength, next set its path for downtown Oak Lawn, Illinois, a densely populated suburb of about fifty-five thousand people that borders the southwestern edge of Chicago.

At about 5:30 p.m., the height of the Friday evening rush hour, the tornado approached the congested intersection of 95th Street and Southwest Highway. As traffic crawled along in the rain, the tornado struck with brutal force. About forty cars were tossed about like toys in the funnel cloud, leaving behind a mangled pile of twisted metal and bleeding casualties. Of the thirty-three people killed in the Oak Lawn tornado, the majority died at that intersection. Next, the twister plowed through a high school and a bus garage, picking up one of the buses and depositing it on top of a house down the street. It weakened slightly for a few blocks but picked up strength once more as it careened through a trailer park and flattened a roller skating rink before it moved on to the suburb of Hometown. There, it knocked over an estimated two hundred monuments in Saint Mary's Cemetery.

Next, its fury still not spent, it tore through the suburb of Evergreen Park, where it once again weakened. After hop-scotching along through factories and apartments, it crossed the Dan Ryan Expressway at 5:35 p.m., flipping a semi truck and scattering some cars. Finally, it skipped out across Lake Michigan, bidding the city goodbye with one-hundred-mile-per-hour gusts recorded at the water filtration plant at 78th Street and the lakefront. The entire episode had lasted less than fifteen minutes, as the twister tore a sixteen-mile-long path of destruction through the southern suburbs.

In the final tally, at least ten tornadoes had ripped across northern Illinois that gray Friday, three of them ranked as deadly F4 tornadoes, with estimated wind speeds of 207–260 miles per hour. The Fujita scale, which rates tornado intensity, lists potential damage from the F4 category as: "Severe damage. Well-constructed houses leveled; structures with weak foundations blown away some distance; cars thrown and large missiles generated. Skyscrapers and high-rises toppled and destroyed."

The storm left 58 people dead and more than 1,500 injured, some critically. Property damage estimates (in today's dollars) exceeded $0.5 billion. The cleanup took weeks, and some reminders—such as crushed farm buildings outside of Belvidere and splintered trees near Lake Zurich—remained for years. It was a long time before most Chicagoans slipped back into complacency. For those who did, an F5 tornado—the only one of that severity ever to hit Illinois—raked through suburban Plainfield in 1990, leaving twenty-nine dead and reminding us all of the capricious power of nature.

Part V
RIOTS AND ANARCHY

The 1968 Democratic National Convention

In a land that's known as Freedom, how can such a thing be fair?
Won't you please come to Chicago for the help that we can bring?
...Won't you please come to Chicago, or else join the other side?
—from "Chicago," lyrics and music by Graham Nash

The year 1968 was a violent and turbulent time in the United States. Antiwar protests festered at colleges and universities across the nation. Civil rights activists marched, often taunted by hostile onlookers. Hippies preached a message of peace and love but all too often ended up in angry clashes with police. And through it all, political parties were plagued by deep divisiveness as they struggled to come to terms with a rapidly changing America.

In April, civil rights leader Martin Luther King Jr. was struck down by an assassin's bullet in Memphis, Tennessee, sparking riots that continued for weeks. James Earl Ray was arrested for the crime and sentenced to ninety-nine years in prison, where he ultimately died of hepatitis in 1998. Ray later recanted his confession, which he claimed had been given under duress. Ray spoke often of conspiracies, but his stories were vague, either because they were false or because he really didn't know exactly what had happened. In any case, King's family believed that he was telling the truth.

Coretta Scott King, Martin Luther's widow, later filed and won a civil wrongful death suit against Loyd Jowers, a Memphis restaurant owner, and "other unknown co-conspirators" for their role in the assassination. Jowers had boasted that he was part of a conspiracy between the Mafia and the U.S. government to assassinate King and said that Ray was simply a scapegoat. Jowers also claimed that Memphis police officer Lieutenant Earl Clark fired the fatal shots. Others have accused the FBI. The controversy around King's death was never put to rest, but no one else was ever charged in the crime. As a result, anger, paranoia and mistrust of the government spread throughout segments of the country.

President Lyndon B. Johnson had originally planned to run for another term of office, but as political unrest and opposition to the Vietnam War grew, Johnson abruptly changed his mind and announced that he would not seek reelection. The war itself seemed to be spiraling out of control, spawning a major rift in the Democratic Party. It would need to find a way to pull together if the party hoped to put forth a candidate able to win the next election. Robert F. "Bobby" Kennedy, the younger brother of assassinated President John F. Kennedy, seemed like the winning choice.

In June, the day after he defeated Eugene McCarthy in the California primary, Bobby Kennedy was also assassinated. He was struck by three bullets fired by Sirhan Sirhan, a Christian Palestinian who supposedly had resented Kennedy's support of Israel during the Six-Day War of 1967. Kennedy died of his injuries the next day. Sirhan was originally sentenced to death, but the sentence was later commuted to life in prison, where he remains today. Kennedy's death was a severe blow to the Democrats, as well as to those who had mourned his brother just five years previously.

As with King's death, conspiracy theorists believed that Sirhan Sirhan was just a dupe for a deeper plot. It was no secret that Kennedy had made enemies. Clyde Tolson, deputy under FBI director J. Edgar Hoover, was once reported as saying, "I hope that someone shoots and kills the son of a bitch." Once again, however, the investigation ended with Sirhan's capture, and no one else was ever formally implicated.

It was against this backdrop of violence, anger and suspicion that the Democrats began to plan their August 1968 convention. The previous year, during a fundraiser for President Johnson's presumed reelection campaign, Chicago's mayor, Richard J. Daley, had extracted a promise from Johnson that the event would be held in Chicago. Daley had been instrumental in bringing out voters and swinging Illinois' twenty-seven electoral votes to Kennedy in the 1960 election, but he was unsure of his ability to pull it off

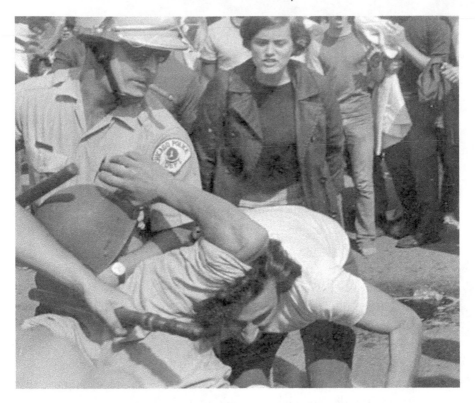

Chicago policeman attacks a legal demonstrator at the 1968 Democratic National Convention in Chicago. *Copyright © by Jo Freeman, www.jofreeman.com.*

again unless he had some way of boosting local voters' confidence. The prestige of bringing the impressive convention to the city, along with all the photo opportunities for Daley while he hobnobbed with national policy makers, would likely help the boss of Chicago politics to reinforce his clout.

As the time neared, antiwar demonstrators, led by such groups as Students for a Democratic Society (SDS) and the National Mobilization Committee to End the War in Vietnam, began to gear up for simultaneous protests. The Youth International Party, or "Yippies," as they were known, also planned a youth festival to coincide with the convention. The Yippies were an antiwar and free speech countercultural group who often employed theatrics to make their point. Due to their media-seeking antics, some of the more intellectual groups distanced themselves a bit, even though they shared many of the same goals.

Mayor Daley, of course, did not want a bunch of angry and media-savvy protestors screwing up his chance to showcase Chicago on a national level and refused to issue permits to most of the groups. Only one small protest in Grant Park was grudgingly sanctioned by the city. In the end, Daley's smoke and mirrors attempt at presenting a happy shiny city was fraught with irony. When delegates arrived at the International Amphitheater, they were greeted by a building that was surrounded by barbed wire and patrolled by armed and helmeted police, while Secret Service agents in dark suits scurried about surreptitiously. The front doors had been bulletproofed, and National Guard troops stood at the ready. Large stockade fences had been hastily erected to block the view of nearby slaughterhouses and run-down neighborhoods as gaily colored flags decorated with flowers and birds whipped in the wind. In the front of this Gestapo-like compound, a huge banner read "Hello Democrats!"

As the convention commenced, protestors began to flow into the city. Minor skirmishes between demonstrators and the police were so frequent that they barely made the news. Some events were tragic and others, downright comedic. Yippie leader Jerry Rubin, folk singer Phil Ochs and other Yippie supporters held a mock nominating convention of their own at Chicago's Civic Center with their prime candidate Pigasus, a live pig. Angry police arrested seven protesters and their porcine nominee, leading evening newscasters to ponder how the pig would make bail.

By August 28, the third day of the convention, no one was laughing. The clashes between police and protestors were growing more frequent and more violent by the hour. With chants of "Hell no, we won't go!" antiwar demonstrators marched in front of the cameras. That afternoon, a young boy at the one legal protest in Grant Park approached a flagpole and began lowering the American flag. With that, police burst through the crowd and began beating the boy. Angry protesters started throwing rocks at the police, who lobbed canisters of tear gas in response.

Tom Hayden, an SDS leader, urged demonstrators to leave the park and fan out through the city, saying that if blood was to be spilled, it should be spilled throughout the city. The protestors surged for the amphitheater and the nearby Hilton Hotel, where most of the delegates were staying. What transpired next was termed a "police riot" by the Walker Report, which was the final report of a commission appointed to investigate the events surrounding the Chicago convention.

The police began to attack the demonstrators and anyone else in the immediate area. Some ripped off their badges and threw them to the ground

Chicago police officers
and Illinois National
Guardsman riot along
with demonstrators
in front of the Hilton
Hotel during the 1968
Democratic National
Convention. *Copyright
© by Jo Freeman, www.
jofreeman.com.*

before charging into the crowds. Many of those targeted were journalists and
photographers, whose cameras and microphones were smashed. According
to the Walker Report:

> *Out of 300 newsmen assigned to cover the parks and streets of Chicago
> during convention week, more than 60 (about 20%) were involved in
> incidents resulting in injury to themselves, damage to their equipment,
> or their arrest. Sixty-three newsmen were physically attacked by police;
> in 13 of these instances, photographic or recording equipment was
> intentionally damaged.*

Innocent bystanders and neighborhood residents were also caught in the riot and often beaten bloody for no cause. By the time the crowd reached the Hilton, the violence was out of control. Mayor Daley's version of the Land of Oz was quickly disintegrating, as sickening images of police brutality raced across television feeds around the globe.

For about twenty minutes, the melee continued under the glare of the media's spotlights as protestors chanted "The whole world is watching!" Police dispersed so much tear gas into the crowd that it began to seep into the convention hall and the Hilton Hotel, where Democratic presidential nominee Hubert Humphrey was bothered by it as he attempted to shower in his room. The night was a blur of rage-twisted faces, bloodied youths and helmeted police and guardsman. Although there was no question that the protestors had greatly antagonized the police, the brutal response didn't gain the department much sympathy. One policeman interviewed by the Walker Commission said, "What happened [that night] didn't have anything to do with police work."

Connecticut senator Abraham Ribicoff decried the violence outside, saying, "With George McGovern [as president] we wouldn't have Gestapo tactics on the streets of Chicago." Mayor Daley's response was swift and laced with profanity. Although his voice wasn't picked up by the television sound crews, it wasn't difficult to deduce at least a portion of what he was saying by reading his lips. News analysts quickly pounced on the exchange as another example of unrest and dissent within the political party. By the time the night was over, Hubert Humphrey had won the Democratic nomination, but his victory was overshadowed by the drama unfolding outside the convention hall.

Ultimately, those disturbing images probably contributed to Humphrey's loss to Richard Nixon in the 1968 presidential election. Nixon's strict, no-nonsense law and order approach was an appealing alternative to the lawlessness and anarchy that had spewed out of Chicago earlier in the year.

Daley, for his part, managed to deflect criticism by maintaining that the police presence was needed due to some vague assassination threats against him and some of the candidates. In the final count, some twenty-three thousand police and National Guardsmen had been on hand to "control" an estimated ten thousand protestors. The 1968 Democratic Convention soon became a symbolic representation of the antiwar and free speech movements, spurring folk songs, books and sociological studies in its wake.

THE HAYMARKET SQUARE RIOT

There will be a time when our silence will be more powerful than the voices you strangle today.

—August Spies, as he stood on the gallows

Chicago has always been a union town. In fact, of the top ten largest cities in the United States, Chicago ranks second only to New York in the percentage of labor force that is unionized. According to recent surveys, about 17.5 percent of city and metropolitan area workers belong to a union. And that's an average—in the public sector, the percentage jumps to an astounding 54.7 percent.

Part of the reason is that Chicago is a city built on industry. As a transportation hub and manufacturing center, the young city drew hundreds of thousands of workers, many of them immigrants with a limited grasp of the culture and language of their new homeland. These people were often forced by necessity into a life of backbreaking labor in order to feed their hungry families. Many business owners exploited the workers, requiring them to work long hours for precious little pay.

It was a story that played out across the city in industries as far-ranging as steel mills, slaughterhouses, wood mills and rail yards: the average employee worked ten to twelve hours per day, six days a week, with no benefits and no paid time off. If one was bold enough to complain, he was simply terminated. Those who suffered physical disabilities from their work were discarded once they were no longer useful or productive. Although some companies might have been compassionate, others were barely a cut above slave masters. Trapped as they were by circumstance, the workers were largely invisible and mute.

In the early 1800s, the Industrial Revolution in Britain triggered a crusade known as the eight-hour-day movement. Socialist Robert Owen first proposed the forty-hour workweek with the slogan "eight hours labour, eight hours recreation, eight hours rest." The idea began to take hold in other industrialized countries, and soon the International Workingmen's Association took up the battle cry. The premise was quickly accepted in Australia, but other countries steadfastly resisted. Labor organizers began to lobby for its adoption, and eventually the Federation of Organized Trades and Labor Unions agreed that May 1, 1886, would

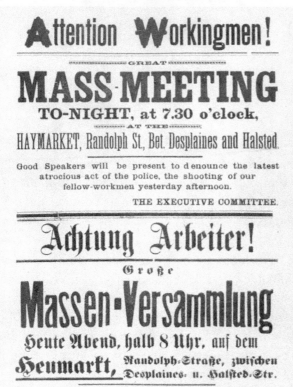

A flyer advertising the planned labor meeting at Haymarket Square.

be the deadline. As the date approached without resolution, a general strike call went out to laborers.

On the first of May, labor unions sponsored assemblies in cities across America. New York, Detroit and Milwaukee each rallied about 10,000 workers. In Chicago, Albert Parsons, founder of the International Working People's Association (IWPA), drew a crowd of more than 80,000, which he and his wife and children led in a march down Michigan Avenue. Parsons was an anarchist who believed that most laws of the government were designed to trample the working class while allowing a de facto ruling class to remain idle. Nearly 340,000 Chicago laborers joined in the strike, crippling businesses and spurring outrage in the press.

Within days, the confrontations turned deadly. On May 3, police fired on a group of striking laborers at the McCormick Harvesting Machine

Company's reaper plant, killing as many as six of them. (Newspaper accounts from the time vary between two and six dead.) In response to the police brutality, Parsons and other fellow anarchists planned a rally for the next day at Haymarket Square, a busy commercial center near the corner of Randolph and Desplaines Streets. Posters were distributed in both English and German, urging workers to come in support of their fallen comrades.

August Spies, one of the core organizers, believed strongly that it should be a peaceful rally. In spite of his circumspect behavior, the police and politicians were ready for a fight. The evening's agenda began with a speech by Spies, who stood addressing the thick horde of attendees from the back of an open wagon. As he glanced around at the large number of armed policemen encircling the crowd, he was quoted as saying:

> [H]*ere seems to prevail the opinion in some quarters that this meeting has been called for the purpose of inaugurating a riot, hence these warlike preparations on the part of so-called "law and order." However, let me tell you at the beginning that this meeting has not been called for any such purpose. The object of this meeting is to explain the general situation of the eight-hour movement and to throw light upon various incidents in connection with it.*

The crowd of about 1,500 was calm and subdued as they listened to the speeches in a drizzling rain. By about 10.30 p.m., the rally was drawing to a close as Samuel Fielden, the last speaker, was winding up his oration. Suddenly, the police began to advance menacingly on the crowd, ordering them to disperse "in the name of the people of Illinois." Without warning, an unknown attacker tossed a crudely made pipe bomb at the cluster of policemen, killing thirty-four-year-old officer Mathias J. Degan. Immediately, the police opened fire on the crowd. Although some of the laborers were indeed armed, it's unclear how many returned fire. The whole confrontation lasted a mere five minutes but left a scene of devastating carnage in its wake. Eight police officers had died, and about sixty had been wounded, mostly from friendly fire.

Casualties among the laborers were harder to determine, in part because the wounded were afraid to seek medical attention for fear of being arrested. At least four civilians died, but some accounts of the day place the number of civilian deaths closer to fifty, with untold more injured. Almost all witnesses

Haymarket Square, scene of the deadly riot.

agreed that the laborers, many of whom were fleeing as the police fired on them, suffered far more losses than the police. The best estimate is about fifty killed and more than one hundred injured. Perhaps the civilian deaths were underreported in the media in an attempt to make the police look more sympathetic. In any case, it was a senseless loss of life on both sides for what had been intended as a peaceful protest.

Immediately after the riot, the police arrested ten men who had been involved with the rally or its organizers and charged them with murder for the bomb-related death of Officer Degan. They were August Spies, Albert Parsons, Adolph Fischer, George Engel, Louis Lingg, Michael Schwab, Samuel Fielden, Oscar Neebe, William Seliger and Rudolph Schnaubelt. Selinger agreed to testify for the prosecution in exchange for the charges against him being dropped, and Schnaubelt fled the country. The remaining eight went to trial, and all were found guilty. Seven of the eight received the death penalty, but Neebe escaped with a fifteen-year sentence.

It was an unusual verdict, especially since some of the men were not even present when the bomb was thrown. The prosecutor's argument was that they had all conspired to create the events that caused the bombing and were thus equally responsible. The spurious court proceedings outraged workers and labor unions, but the press mostly demonized the men. The event had a polarizing effect that was felt around the world; the defendants were folk heroes in certain circles but "filthy anarchists" and "demons" in others.

Eventually, after lengthy appeals, Governor Richard Oglesby commuted Michael Schwab and Samuel Fielden's sentences to life in prison. The rest of the men were scheduled for execution on November 11, 1887, but Louis Lingg committed suicide in his jail cell the night before. He held a smuggled dynamite cap in his mouth and lit the fuse. Unfortunately, the blast didn't kill him instantly, and he died a slow, agonizing death over the course of several hours.

On the appointed day, the remaining four were marched to the gallows at the Criminal Courts Building on Hubbard Street. They were garbed in white robes and hoods and remained defiant until the end. Their demise was not a quick one; witnesses stated that the men slowly strangled to death in a gruesome manner. Lucy Parsons attended the execution to catch a final glimpse of her husband, but she was arrested and searched for bombs or weapons. Of course, she had none.

Officer Mathias J. Degan was killed when a bomb was thrown at police during a labor rally.

In 1893, Illinois governor John Altgeld pardoned the remaining defendants. He characterized the trial as a travesty of justice and accused the presiding judge of being clearly biased in favor of the prosecution. The convicted men were never proven to be guilty of the crime for which they were charged, and the jury was hand-picked by state prosecutors with jurors who were obviously opposed to the labor movement.

But who did throw the bomb? The list of suspects is nearly limitless, and historians have never agreed on the culprit. Some point the finger at Rudolph Schnaubelt, who fled before trial, but there is no real proof against him. Others blame Pinkerton guards, who had been hired by McCormick to guard the plant and police the striking workers. The Pinkertons or another "agent provocateur" might have been acting to incite the riot and discredit the labor movement. Yet others blame a mysterious stranger who purportedly hinted to a saloon keeper in Indianapolis that he was heading to Chicago to make trouble for the anarchists.

Most likely is Governor Altgeld's theory, that "the bomb was, in all probability, thrown by someone seeking personal revenge." There was certainly enough anger building against the government and its police forces

Depiction of police firing into crowd at Haymarket labor rally as bomb explodes.

to incite someone to act out. Unfortunately, the least likely suspects are the five men who actually died for the crime and the three others who spent many years in prison.

In 1889, the city placed a statue on the site to commemorate the policemen who died. It was eventually moved to the Chicago Police Academy after repeated bombings and acts of vandalism caused severe damage. A Haymarket martyr's memorial in Waldheim Cemetery in Forest Park commemorates the activists who were buried there after their execution. And finally, in 2004, the City of Chicago commissioned a statue by sculptor Mary Brogger that depicts the scene from that deadly night, including the open wagon on which the organizers stood. Sadly, both the memorial at the cemetery and the plaque next to Brogger's sculpture have been vandalized, just as the police statue before them. Even after 125 years, the unrest and divisiveness between labor and business continue to haunt us like the ghosts of those long-dead martyrs.

THE E2 NIGHTCLUB STAMPEDE

I'm at a loss for words…we shouldn't be burying a twenty-two-year-old because she went out to a club.

—stepfather of victim Nicole Patterson

Sunday, February 16, 2003, was a typical blustery winter day in Chicago. A frigid northeast wind gusted across Lake Michigan as gray clouds scuttled through the sky. The temperature hadn't risen out of the twenties all weekend, and the threat of a snowstorm like the one that was pounding the eastern seaboard hung in the air. Chicago residents were used to capricious weather, however, and wouldn't allow their plans to be hampered by the possibility of a mere snowstorm. Besides, the next day was Presidents Day, which meant an extra-long weekend for many workers, just perfect for a little mid-winter socializing to break up the doldrums.

For many young people on Chicago's near South Side, the trendy E2 nightclub on the second floor of 2347 South Michigan was the place to go. The sixteen-thousand-square-foot landmark building had once housed a car dealership and was still in fact owned by Lesly Motors, but it had long ago been transformed into a restaurant and club. Friday had been Valentine's

Day, and the Epitome Restaurant downstairs was filled with couples enjoying a romantic, if somewhat pricey, dinner of steak or seafood; by Sunday night, it was singles out for an evening of clubbing that filled the upstairs night spot. Unfortunately, E2 wasn't even supposed to be in existence anymore.

E2 was just the latest incarnation in a series of nightclubs at the site. Its predecessors included La Mirage, Heroes and The Clique, all popular destinations for urban young adults. Chicago FM radio station WGCI had hosted events there with such popular entertainers as Destiny's Child and Alicia Keys. Its clientele was equally impressive: Cuba Gooding Jr. and Sean "Diddy" Combs showed up to dance and drink, and boxer Mike Tyson

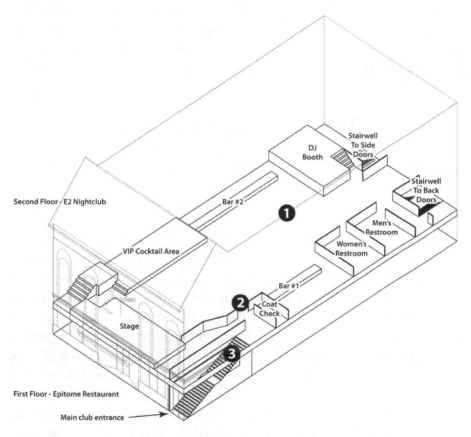

Floor plan of the E2 Nightclub. 1) security guards used pepper spray to break up a fight on the dance floor; 2) frightened crowds trying to escape the noxious fumes surged for the single marked exit; 3) people fell or were pushed down the narrow staircase and trampled in the panic. Some reports say that security guards locked the main club entrance in an effort to slow the crowd, resulting in a crush of trapped bodies.

was arrested there after being accused of assaulting a young woman. Elroy Smith, the program director at WGCI, summed it up like this: "It's a known landmark in Chicago. Mention E2 to anyone in the African American community and they know about it. It's not your average nightclub."

The Chicago Police Department and city inspectors also knew all too well about the club. In the two years prior to the disaster, police had been called to the location about eighty times to break up fights or respond to gunshots outside. City building inspectors had cited the owners, Dwain Kyles and Calvin Hollins Jr., for at least eleven building code violations and had ordered the club closed in 2002. Some of the violations included failure to provide enough exits, overcrowding and insufficient or nonworking emergency exit lighting. Later, lawyers for Kyles and Hollins disputed that the club had ever been ordered to close and cited the venue's frequent and aggressive advertising as proof that the city must have been aware that it was still operating.

According to the city, however, inspectors were only aware that the downstairs Epitome restaurant was open and believed that the club had been shut down. The periodic health and building inspections of the Epitome had usually been carried out during the daytime, when the upstairs club was not open, but Fire Commissioner James Joyce of Chicago later claimed that five routine inspections during 2002 had been carried out on weekend nights, and the club was closed and dark each time.

In any event, the club was indeed operating that cold February night, and nearly record crowds had turned out to listen to the hip-hop tracks and dance mixes being played by Clear Channel Communications deejay Vaughn Woods. Estimates of the crowd vary wildly, with some sources claiming that 1,500 people were crammed into the small room that evening and other sources pegging the number as low as 500 people. The most reliable estimate is the grand jury indictment in the case, which stated that about 1,200 people were present on the night of the stampede, roughly five times the club's capacity of 240. Whatever the true number, everyone in attendance agreed that it was unusually crowded and hot that night. The small dance floor was packed, and sweaty patrons had to struggle through crowds to reach the long black marble bar for another Bacardi or apple martini. At twenty dollars per person cover charge, and with drinks selling for five to ten dollars each, it promised to be a profitable night for the owners.

Shortly after 2:00 a.m. Monday morning, a fight broke out between two women on the dance floor. One reportedly was wielding a box cutter, and burly security guards moved in to break it up. Soon, others jumped into the fray and it became a brawl. In an effort to restore order, the guards began to spray participants with pepper spray. At first, the disturbance went unnoticed in other areas of the club. Deejay Woods even joked about it, saying, "They ain't going to stop this party" and "Next week, half-price admission if y'all bring your own gas mask!" As the pepper spray began to concentrate in the dark, crowded and poorly ventilated room, however, people began to cough and vomit. Many in the club weren't aware of the source of the noxious fumes and began to panic. In the post-9/11 urban area, fears of terrorist chemical attacks ran high, and someone shouted "I'll bet it's [Osama] bin Laden!"

Although the club actually had three exits—front, side and rear—they were either unmarked or unlit, and some survivors claimed that the rear and side exits were locked during the early phase of the disaster. Frightened patrons rushed for the only exit they knew: the steep front stairs through which they'd entered earlier. To make matters worse, the doors on that stairwell opened inward, one of the many fire code violations listed when the club was supposedly ordered closed. The steps leading down to those doors were narrow, dark and treacherous, and people began to fall as the surging crowd pressed forward.

Inside the club, it was complete bedlam. The deejay continued to play music and tried to calm the throngs, but the suffocating fumes threw people into a blind panic. Many fainted, while others vomited or screamed in terror for assistance. Even those who had remained calm were swept along helplessly by the sea of people pushing for the single narrow exit. Soon, the stairwell was filled with fallen bodies as a human avalanche continued to flow down the steps. The crowd was no longer a group of individuals, but rather had turned into a seething and writhing beast, completely out of control.

Many witnesses claim that security guards initially locked the front door in an attempt to slow the crowd, but their effort just had the effect of worsening the pileup and causing more casualties. By the time police and fire rescue teams arrived, they were greeted with the horrendous sight of bloodied and trampled bodies pressed against the glass doors and piled over six feet high at the base of the stairwell. Rescuers ran up the side and rear stairwells (at least one of which had been reportedly chained shut) to guide some of the remaining club-goers away from the front exit and safely out of the building, while emergency responders tried to untangle the mass of living, dead and injured at the front entrance.

Exterior of the Epitome Restaurant and E2 Nightclub after the disaster.

One of the first doctors to arrive was an emergency room physician from Northwestern Memorial Hospital named Dr. Christopher Beach. He had been told that there were mass casualties and an unknown vapor, and he initially believed that he was responding to a terrorist attack. "It was a very scary scene," he later related. While Dr. Beach and others began the grim task of triaging injuries and casualties, friends and family of those still trapped paced anxiously on the sidewalk, hoping to catch sight of their loved ones. Eventually, police asked all bystanders to disperse and clear the street for medical and rescue personnel. Many continued their odyssey of hope by visiting area hospitals, praying that they would find the person they sought being treated for minor injuries.

By the gray dawn of morning, twenty-one families knew that their loved ones would not be returning home. In the final tally, twelve women and nine men between the ages of twenty-one and forty-three died from "compressional asphyxiation," a rather sterile term for death by crushing and suffocation. Scores were injured, and many victims were hospitalized with injuries ranging from severe bruising and sprains up to broken bones and head injuries. As the families began to grieve, outraged politicians and the media began to demand answers as to why and how the tragedy occurred. A row of twenty-one small white wooden crosses inscribed with names and ages bore silent witness against the alley wall of the building where the needless deaths occurred, and passersby added flowers, balloons, photos and personal notes to the memorial. The following Sunday, February 23, local churches rang their bells twenty-one times at noon to pay tribute to the victims, as Mayor Daley promised justice.

The city quickly brought criminal charges of involuntary manslaughter against owners Dwain Kyles and Calvin Hollins Jr. and, later, against promoter Marco Flores and club manager Calvin Hollins III. Hollins Jr. and Kyles were also charged with contempt of court in a separate Housing Court case accusing them of violating an order to close E2 because of building code violations. In addition, victims soon filed more than sixty civil lawsuits against the club's owners, managers, promoters and Clear Channel Communications, which employed the deejay that provided entertainment that night.

When the criminal cases finally wound through court, all of the defendants were acquitted of involuntary manslaughter. In 2009, Kyles and Hollins Jr. were each sentenced to two years in prison on charges of indirect criminal contempt for operating the club in defiance of the ordered closing. Lawyers for the defendants claimed that the owners had "misunderstood" the closing order, believing that it referred to an elevated skybox in the nightclub and not to the nightclub in its entirety. The judge also ordered that $2.5 million of assets be set aside in a special fund in anticipation of the civil lawsuits. As of this writing, Kyles and Hollins are appealing their sentences, and the civil cases continue to trudge slowly through the court system.

Both E2 and the Epitome Restaurant closed after the incident, and the building sits vacant. The crosses have long since disappeared, and little remains to tell the story of that tragic night and the twenty-one promising lives snuffed out because of greed and carelessness.

ABOUT THE AUTHOR

Gayle Soucek is an author and freelance editor, with several books and numerous magazine articles to her credit, including *Marshall Field's: The Store that Helped Build Chicago*, published by The History Press. She once served as managing editor for the Chicago art and entertainment biweekly *Nightmoves* and is a current contributing writer for www.webvet.com.

Gayle is a lifelong Chicagoan and Blackhawks hockey fan. She resides in the western suburbs with her photographer husband, dogs, parrots, reptiles and one very laid-back cat. One of her favorite pastimes is exploring the Windy City, with its fascinating culture, beautiful architecture and weird and wonderful history.

Visit us at
www.historypress.net

CPSIA information can be obtained
at www.ICGtesting.com
Printed in the USA
LVHW07*2157240518
578381LV00021B/284/P

9 781540 220981